Led by the Holy Spirit

Led
by the
Holy
Spirit

Katie Lopez

Debarim Publishing
807 W Broadway St.
Spiro, OK 74959
www.debarimpublishing.com

Paperback ISBN-13: 979-8-9924767-7-4
Ebook ISBN-13: 979-8-9924767-8-1

Preface

The past two years have been challenging for me and my husband as we have been processing the loss of our infant son, James. He was stillborn around week thirty-seven. We prayed for resurrec-tion, but the Father said to let go. By His grace, we drew closer to Him through this immense trial, allowing Him to shape and mold us. However, during the initial weeks and months following James' death, I wrestled with His answer to our request for resurrection.

Father, why did You say, "Let go," when Your Word says we will be raising the dead? (Matthew 10:8, Mark 16:17-18). *Lord, we were trying to obey Your Word and bring him back…*

The Holy Spirit answered gently with this Bible verse.

> *For as many as are led by the Spirit of God, these are sons of God.* (Romans 8:14 NKJV)

The Passion Translation says,

> *The **mature** children of God are those who are moved by the impulses of the Holy Spirit.* (Romans 8:14)

There was deep revelation in this simple verse. In fact, it was the catalyst that led me to write this book. The impression from the Holy Spirit was that even with a command in Scripture like *cast out demons, heal the sick, and raise the dead,* the mature children of God will still ask,

Do You want to raise this person from the dead, Lord? Do You want to heal this person, Lord? How are You moving in this situation so I can join You?

The scales began to fall from my spiritual eyes and heart. What seemed like a *huge* contradiction was not at all. Yes, the Lord will raise the dead and heal the sick through His followers, *but only as the Holy Spirit leads.* As mature followers of the Messiah, we must learn to be led by the Holy Spirit in all things.

Over the following months, as I allowed this new concept to mar-inate in my heart, the Holy Spirit began giving me opportunities to be led by Him like never before. As I obeyed, my striving to please God stopped. In fact, I didn't even realize I had been striving for years until the Lord showed me this mature way of being led by His Spirit daily. My acts of love toward others began to be Spirit-led, filling me and others with joy. I was no longer trying to help whoever, whenever and feeling exhausted, wondering if I was making a difference in God's Kingdom. This child-like obedience in being led by His Spirit was refreshing and bore good fruit, while allowing me to enter a special rest with Him I never knew before!

So then we must be eager to experience this faith-rest life,
so that no one falls short by following the same pattern
of doubt and unbelief. (Hebrews 4:11)

During this season, the Father also showed me examples from Scripture of Yeshua and His followers being led by the Holy Spirit in similar ways. I'm excited to share these examples from Scripture and many personal testimonies of being led by the Holy Spirit as well. I'm finding that being led by the Holy Spirit daily increases our matu-rity in the Messiah, allowing us to bear richer and greater fruit for the Kingdom of Heaven.

> *I am the true Vine, and My Father is the vinedresser. Every branch in Me that does not bear fruit, He takes away; and every branch that continues to bear fruit, He [repeatedly] prunes, so that it will bear more fruit [even richer and finer fruit].* (John 15:1-2 AMP)

Note to the Reader

Throughout the book, you will notice I use Jesus' Aramaic name, Yeshua, instead of His English translated name, Jesus.

I enjoy when folks use my real name instead of a translation of it. So, I prefer to call Him Yeshua, to show Him honor and love in the same way.

I understand there are various pronunciations and spellings of Yeshua. From my current research and understanding, I believe this version to be the closest. However, if you disagree, I pray you are able to cover it in grace as you read along.

Dedication

I dedicate this book to my Father in Heaven.

He is my life.

May the Scriptures and testimonies in these pages draw you closer to Him.

Table of Contents

Chapter 1

How Yeshua Was Led

After the Lord showed me that the mature sons of God are led by the Holy Spirit (Romans 8:14), I began searching the Scriptures to discover mature followers of the Messiah who were led by the Holy Spirit. As I studied, it dawned on me that perhaps I should begin with Yeshua Himself. He modeled following the Holy Spirit and the Father beautifully.

When I was younger, I read Bible verses that spoke of how Yeshua obeyed the Holy Spirit and the Father perfectly. Over the years, I just assumed since Yeshua was a form of God in the flesh, that following the Holy Spirit for Him was easy. Recently however, the Lord showed me that Yeshua's obedience was a choice. He had His own will (Luke 22:42), and He was also tempted to sin, but chose not to (Hebrews 4:15).

> *He existed in the form of God, yet he gave no thought to seizing equality with God as his supreme prize. Instead he emptied himself of his outward glory by reducing himself to the form of a lowly servant. He became human!*
>
> *He humbled himself and became vulnerable, choosing to be revealed as a man and was obedient. He was a perfect*

1

example, even in his death—a criminal's death by cruci-
fixion! (Philippians 2:6-8)

For we do not have a High Priest who is unable to sym-
pathize and understand our weaknesses and temptations,
but One who has been tempted [knowing exactly how it
feels to be human] in every respect as we are, yet without
[committing any] sin. (Hebrews 4:15 AMP)

In addition, Scripture says that Yeshua grew naturally in wisdom
and in maturity, and still, He never sinned.

As Jesus grew, so did his wisdom and maturity. The favor
of men increased upon his life, for he was greatly loved
by God. (Luke 2:52)

Many passages in Scripture record Yeshua not speaking or doing
things on His own, but only by the Spirit or the Father's will (Matthew
4:1, John 5:19, John 6:38, and John 12:49). As I pondered this amazing
feat, I wondered,
Are followers of the Messiah to only speak and do things by the
Spirit and the Father as well?
It seemed the Lord was listening into my thoughts as He
answered, *Yes!*

For I have never spoken on My own initiative or authority,
but the Father Himself who sent Me has given Me a com-
mandment regarding what to say and what to speak. (John
12:49 AMP)

I'm Ready to Mature

Especially after what we had just gone through with baby James, I longed to understand more about how Yeshua flowed with Holy Spirit. In our own efforts to raise James from the dead, we exhausted ourselves and our emotions were raw. Had we originally tuned into what Holy Spirit was saying, (to let go) we could have saved ourselves the additional heartache of trying to bring him back.

As I pondered the gravity of being led by the Holy Spirit in all things, I began to extrapolate,

In the past, had I tried to heal people or cast out demons in my own strength or timing without the leading of the Holy Spirit? Is that why sometimes people were not healed or sometimes the demons came back? I wasn't being led?

My mind was reeling now. There are actual Bible verses where Yeshua warns us not to cast out demons prematurely or it will make it worse for the person (Matthew 12:43-45). Yikes! It's definitely time to mature.

As the Lord led me to research various Scriptures and stories in the Bible, He showed me that in order to be successful in healing the sick, raising the dead, cleansing the lepers, casting out demons, and so on, we must be led by the Holy Spirit like Yeshua was. It's not the wisest use of our energy to attempt things on our own, hoping for the best. Instead, if we are led by the Holy Spirit, He will activate the gifts within us and lead us to use our authority at just the right time.

> *Remember, it is the same Holy Spirit who distributes, activates, and operates these different gifts as he chooses for each believer.* (1 Corinthians 12:11)

As I continued to study the Scriptures, the Lord guided me to write this book using the life of the Messiah and His followers as our example of being led. He also encouraged me to include testimonies from my own life as they related to each topic.

I have done my best to group the concepts together into chapters, including Bible verses for support. Many of the concepts I have experienced personally, but others are newer to me. I'm not saying I have arrived, but I have definitely matured from what the Lord has shown me and am producing much better fruit because of it. It's getting easier for me to be led by the Holy Spirit daily, to recognize His voice, and to understand the ways He communicates. Lord willing, the concepts will be helpful to you as well.

Chapter 2

Led to be Baptized with the Holy Spirit

Using Yeshua as our example, one of the first things we see Him doing is getting baptized by water in the Jordon River and also getting baptized with the Holy Spirit. Scripture says Yeshua was overflowing with the Holy Spirit from this point on.

> One day, Jesus came to be baptized along with all the others. As he was consumed with the spirit of prayer, the heavenly realm ripped open above him and the Holy Spirit descended from heaven in the form of a dove and landed on him. Then God's audible voice was heard, saying,
>
> "My Son, you are my beloved one. Through you I am fulfilled."
>
> From the moment of his baptism, Jesus overflowed with the Holy Spirit. (Luke 3:21-22 & Luke 4:1)

To follow Yeshua's example, believers should be baptized in water and also baptized with the Holy Spirit. The baptism of the Holy Spirit is a gift from the Father for all believers. Before Yeshua left the earth, He explained to His followers that they should have both baptisms.

> **The baptism of the Holy Spirit is a gift from the Father for all believers.**

*Jesus instructed them, "Don't leave Jerusalem, but wait here until you receive the gift I told you about, **the gift the Father has promised**. For John baptized you in water, but in a few days from now you will be baptized in the Holy Spirit!"* (Acts 1:4-5)

Yeshua likened the baptism of the Holy Spirit to being clothed with power from on high. It was so important that His followers receive the power of the Holy Spirit, that Yeshua commanded them to wait for it.

Listen carefully: I am sending the Promise of My Father [the Holy Spirit] upon you; but you are to remain in the city [of Jerusalem] until you are clothed (fully equipped) with power from on high. (Luke 24:49 AMP)

> **Yeshua likened the baptism of the Holy Spirit to being clothed with power from on high.**

Yeshua's followers were faithful to wait. Praise the Lord!

On the day Pentecost was being fulfilled, all the disciples were gathered in one place. Suddenly they heard the sound of a violent blast of wind rushing into the house from out of the heavenly realm. The roar of the wind was so overpowering it was all anyone could bear!

Then all at once a pillar of fire appeared before their eyes. It separated into tongues of fire that engulfed each one of them.

They were all filled and equipped with the Holy Spirit and were inspired to speak in tongues—empowered by the Spirit to speak in languages they had never learned! (Acts 2:1-4)

The Baptism of the Holy Spirit

Some of you may be familiar with the baptism of the Holy Spirit, while others may not be. In fact, some of you may have grown up with a family member or pastor who spoke against the baptism of the Holy Spirit (gifts of the Spirit, tongues, and so on). Or maybe you were taught it was only for "back then." I speak freely on this topic because I was raised with this exact message growing up – that it was for "back then." Over the years however, the Lord has gently guided me to the truth.

The Baptism of the Holy Spirit

According to Scripture, the baptism of the Holy Spirit is not just for "back then." My personal testimony of being baptized in the Holy Spirit is coming up. But first, let's break it down a little more.

> According to Scripture, the baptism of the Holy Spirit is not just for "back then."

When we are unsure what a word means in our English Bibles, we can search for its definition in a book called the Strongs Concordance. The Strongs Concordance tells us the original Greek or Hebrew definition of the word that was translated into English. Studying the Bible in this way has helped me grow and mature immensely! I use the online version, but there are hard copies as well. It helps you get to the bottom of controversial or hard-to-understand passages by showing you what the original author meant. I highly recommend using the Strongs Concordance as you study the Bible and pursue the Lord and His truth.

So, from the verse in Luke 24:49, "power from on high" the word power here is the Greek word G1411 *dunamis,* and has several meanings:

The baptism of the Holy Spirit brings the believer in Yeshua power or *dunamis*:

a. Strength, ability, power
b. Power for performing miracles
c. Moral power and excellence of soul
d. The power and influence which belong to riches
e. The power consisting in or resting upon armies, forces, and hosts

Every person who is baptized with the Holy Spirit can manifest some or all the above as they are led by the Holy Spirit. During Pentecost, the Holy Spirit baptized many of Yeshua's followers who were Jewish, but here Peter witnesses the Holy Spirit coming upon the Gentiles as well.

> *While Peter was speaking, the Holy Spirit cascaded over all those listening to his message.*
>
> *The Jewish brothers who had accompanied Peter were astounded that the gift of the Holy Spirit was poured out on people who weren't Jews, for they heard them speaking in supernaturally given languages and passionately praising God.* (Acts 10:44-46)
>
> *"Then I remembered the word of the Lord, how He used to say, 'John baptized with water, but you will be baptized with the Holy Spirit.'*
>
> *So, if God gave Gentiles the same gift [equally] as He gave us after we accepted and believed and trusted in the Lord Jesus Christ [as Savior], who was I to interfere or stand in God's way?"* (Acts 11:16-17 AMP)

Here we see the baptism of the Holy Spirit is for everyone who puts their faith in Yeshua (Jew or Gentile).

Now let's see what happened after many of Yeshua's follower received the baptism of the Holy Spirit. What did they do with this power? How did Holy Spirit lead them in this?

11

The apostles performed many signs, wonders, and miracles among the people. And the believers were wonderfully united as they met regularly in the temple courts in the area known as Solomon's Porch. No one dared harm them, for everyone held them in high regard.

Continually more and more people believed in the Lord and were added to their number — great crowds of both men and women.

In fact, when people knew Peter was going to walk by, they carried the sick out to the streets and laid them down on cots and mats, knowing the incredible power emanating from him would overshadow them and heal them.

Great numbers of people swarmed into Jerusalem from the nearby villages. They brought with them the sick and those troubled by demons — and everyone was healed! (Acts 5:12-16)

Wow! This sounds just like Yeshua's ministry. It sounds like maturity in the Messiah. There are so many passages that talk of Yeshua's followers (not just apostles) being led by the Holy Spirit with this power. We will cover more of these examples in Scripture throughout the book, but Abba wants all His followers to have this power and to live dynamically for Him and His Kingdom. Remember, He asked *all* His followers to wait for it (Luke 24:49).

*Whoever believes the good news and is baptized will be saved, and whoever does not believe the good news will be condemned. **And these miracle signs will accompany those who believe**: They will drive out demons in the power of my name. They will speak in tongues. They will be supernaturally protected from snakes and from drinking anything poisonous. And they will lay hands on the sick and heal them.*

After saying these things, Jesus was lifted up into heaven and sat down at the place of honor at the right hand of God!

And the apostles went out announcing the good news everywhere, as the Lord himself consistently worked with them, validating the message they preached with miracle-signs that accompanied them! (Mark 16:16-20)

My Testimony of Being Baptized with the Holy Spirit

When I was young, I asked Yeshua into my heart and was also baptized in water as an outward testimony of my decision to follow the Messiah. Later in my twenties, the Lord led me to a church that believed in the gifts of the Holy Spirit.

Shortly thereafter, I asked the Father to baptize me with the Holy Spirit all by myself in my room. Waiting and wondering, I began to hear syllables and sounds in my heart. By faith, I started speaking them out. The sounds were not English, I knew I was speaking in an inspired tongue from the Holy Spirit – just like I had read about in Scripture! Hallelujah!

At that point, it felt like a whole new world opened up to me. One of the main things that changed in my heart was my boldness to share the gospel. Prior to being baptized in the Holy Spirit, telling others about Yeshua was hard for me. I was never quite sure when to speak about the Lord and when not to. After being baptized in the Holy Spirit, my courage and love toward others increased exponentially. Now when Holy Spirit leads me, it is quite easy to pray with total strangers and to tell them about the Father's love.

> **After being baptized in the Holy Spirit, my courage and love toward others increased exponentially.**

*Now when the men of the Sanhedrin (Jewish High Court) saw the **confidence and boldness** of Peter and John, and grasped the fact that they were uneducated and untrained [ordinary] men, they were astounded, and began to recognize that they had been with Jesus.* (Acts 4:13 AMP)

After being baptized in the Holy Spirit, various gifts began to awaken inside of me as well. One of the gifts (tongues) came right away, while others came later after I matured in the Lord a bit (words of wisdom, words of knowledge, and healing). I also became very sensitive to my dreams, and the Lord began to speak through them to guide me and my family. The Holy Spirit gives gifts to individual believers as *He* wills. We do not all receive the same gifts when we are baptized with the Holy Spirit.

Remember, it is the same Holy Spirit who distributes, activates, and operates these different gifts as he chooses for each believer. (1 Corinthians 12:11)

It is so important to use whatever gifts God has given you as He leads you. The more obedient I am with what I've been given, the more God seems to give me. All glory to God!

For to everyone who has [and values his blessings and gifts from God, and has used them wisely], more will be given, and [he will be richly supplied so that] he will have an abundance; but from the one who does not have [because he has ignored or disregarded his blessings and gifts from God], even what he does have will be taken away. (Matthew 25:29 AMP)

Over the years, the Lord has also brought forth a strong teaching ministry from within me. Paul mentions the different kinds of ministry gifts: apostle, prophet, pastor, teacher, evangelist (1 Corinthians 12 and Ephesians 4).

It is the same Holy Spirit who continues to distribute many different varieties of gifts. The Lord Yahweh is one, and he is the one who apportions to believers different varieties of ministries. (1 Corinthians 12:4-5)

Additionally, I've noticed the baptism of the Holy Spirit brings an overwhelming love for others. It is easier now for me to love others deeply, give them grace, assume the best in them, and forgive them. We see this love reflected in the early church as well.

> *All the believers were one in mind and heart. Selfishness was not a part of their community, for they shared every-thing they had with one another.* (Acts 4:32)

The baptism of the Holy Spirit brings an overwhelming love for others.

Your Turn

If you are seeking maturity in the Messiah, I strongly recommend asking to receive the baptism of the Holy Spirit if you have not yet received it. As you can see from Scripture and from my personal tes-timony, it is not just for "back then." It will help you and will further God's Kingdom *through* you. Your loving Heavenly Father wants you to have it. Yeshua called it a gift. Will you receive it? If so, please agree with the prayer below and mean it in your heart.

"Heavenly Father, I want everything You have for me. Please bap-tize me with the power of the Holy Spirit!"

> *But I promise you this—the Holy Spirit will come upon you, and you will be seized with power. You will be my messengers to Jerusalem, throughout Judea, the dis-tant provinces —even to the remotest places on earth!* (Acts 1:8)

Chapter 3

Led to be Tested

As I continued studying the life of the Messiah as our template in being led by the Holy Spirit, I saw that after Yeshua was baptized, He was immediately led by the Holy Spirit into the desert to be tested by satan (Matthew 4:1). There was purpose for Yeshua to be tested in the desert. I believe Father God wanted to make sure Yeshua's relationship with Him was solid as a rock, so that nothing would sway Him.

The Lord tested His followers in similar ways. In the Book of Deuteronomy, the Lord led the children of Israel into the desert to test their character and to see if they would obey Him. In the Book of Job, the Lord allowed Job to be tested by the devil in many ways. In both cases, the Lord wanted to see how His people would respond. Would they remain faithful to Him? If you are going through a test or a trial right now, please trust the Father has a purpose for it, and do not forsake Him.

> *And we know that all things work together for good to those who love God, to those who are the called according to His purpose.* (Romans 8:28 NKJV)

After going through several dark valleys and tests of our own, I began to understand how the Lord allows testing and trials to check our roots and see how deeply we will go with Him. Will we hold onto Father God when our life is falling to pieces around us? Will we keep trusting Him? Or will we push Him away because of what He allowed to happen in our lives?

> **If you are going through a test or a trial right now, please trust the Father has a purpose for it, and do not forsake Him.**

My Test

Having just lived through the biggest test of my life — losing baby James almost full-term — I actually *told* God He went too far. I was hurt. Angry. Crushed. The conversation went something like this:

Miscarriage after miscarriage is one thing, God – that was painful enough, but now this? You allowed James to go to heaven too? He was basically full term, God! Thirty-seven weeks, 7 pounds 19 inches. He could have lived!

God, You went too far this time! I am broken inside and out. I have no idea how I will ever recover from his death. Abba, where are You in all this!?

I wanted to believe God was good. Deep down I knew He was, but the current facts made things so hard to reconcile. In those hot moments of mine, God didn't say much. Days and weeks passed. I hadn't totally shut Him out, I just didn't understand His ways. Finally, when I was ready to listen to His side of things, He showed me this verse.

To grant to those who mourn in Zion the following: to give them a turban instead of dust [on their heads, a sign of mourning], the oil of joy instead of mourning, the garment [expressive] of praise instead of a disheartened spirit.

*So they will be called the trees of righteousness [strong and magnificent, distinguished for integrity, justice, and right standing with God], **the planting of the Lord, that He may be glorified**.* (Isaiah 61:3 AMP)

The part that stood out to me was being a tree of righteousness and being planted of the Lord so He would get the glory. In other words, as we go through these tests and trials, the Lord is firming up our roots *in Him* so we can be strong, magnificent trees, planted by the Lord. Nothing on earth should be able to sway us from the love of the Father, and because of this, He will get all the glory.

> Nothing on earth should be able to sway us from the love of the Father.

Looking back on it now, I know my roots went deep with Abba through the pain of losing James. The Father encouraged me to sing to Him often, even when I didn't feel like it. This was extremely healing, and by His grace, I also began to thank Him for anything I could think of. This softened my heart towards Him. He was holding onto me, when I wanted to let go of life itself. By God's grace, I finally chose to accept what God allowed to happen with James, without receiving an explanation or reconciliation from Him.

> ### He was holding onto me,
> ### when I wanted to let go of life itself.

I chose to believe in my heart that Abba was still a good God and that He loved me. Once I chose to trust God with this childlike faith, the peace that passes all understanding guarded my heart and my mind. God's peace *passed* my understanding. It jumped right over that part of my brain, allowing me not to need an explanation from Abba, and peace followed.

> *Don't be pulled in different directions or worried about a thing. Be saturated in prayer throughout each day, offering your faith-filled requests before God with over-flowing gratitude. Tell him every detail of your life, then God's wonderful peace that transcends human under-standing, will guard your heart and mind through Jesus Christ.* (Philippians 4:6-7)

Now and then my husband and I can see glimpses of Kingdom fruit from James' death. Our perspective of what is important in life has truly changed. We do not hold onto this world tightly anymore. In addition, as we have received comfort from the Lord in our grief, we can now comfort others who have experienced similar loss. It is bittersweet, but even so, we are able to give God the glory.

> *He always comes alongside us to comfort us in every suf-fering so that we can come alongside those who are in any painful trial. We can bring them this same comfort that God has poured out upon us.* (2 Corinthians 1:4)

We Must Stay Focused

At times, it's hard to know whether we are being led into testing from the Lord, temptations from satan, or something else from this fallen world. Whatever the case, we must not be discouraged, and we must not allow others to make us think something is wrong with us. Quite the opposite – when a believer is seriously living for Yeshua, that is when I have seen the enemy attack the most.

My husband and I have withstood many tests and trials over the years, and we have learned that it is *so* important to remain soft and humble in our hearts towards the Lord. By admitting we do not know everything, we are allowing the Lord to shape and mold us through the trial or the test into what *He* wants us to be.

> When a believer is seriously living for Yeshua, that is when I have seen the enemy attack the most.

It is really important to remain soft and forgiving towards others as well. We must choose not to get offended or stay offended with others who have hurt us or treated us unfairly. We do not have to trust them or remain friends with them, but we absolutely must forgive them.

Later Peter approached Jesus and said, "How many times do I have to forgive my fellow believer who keeps offending me? Seven times?"

Jesus answered, "Not seven times, Peter, but seventy times seven times!" (Matthew 18:21-22)*

** There is a note in The Passion Translation that 70x7 is
a metaphor for limitless forgiveness.*

And just to demonstrate how serious Abba is about forgiving others, He had Yeshua emphasize it to His disciples and others present.

But if you withhold forgiveness from others, your Father withholds forgiveness from you. (Matthew 6:15)

Breathe Into the Contractions

Something I have learned about tests is to breathe into them. Years ago, when giving birth to my first or second child, I remember a nurse or my doula saying something like,

"You must accept the pain of the contractions, Katie. Stop fighting them by holding your breath. Breathe into each contraction. Accept the pain. The pain is bringing your baby into this world."

Very upset at first, I wanted to give that nurse a piece of my mind (terrible, I know – God has done a lot of maturing in me over the years), but then I realized she was right. As I began to breathe into each contraction, although very painful, I made more progress towards delivering my baby.

The same sentiment is true for followers of the Messiah. We must not shy away from the pain of being tested. We must breathe into the testing-contractions. Our Heavenly Father wants to see where we are spiritually. Can He trust us with more? Can He give us more responsibility in His Kingdom? Will we remain faithful to Him if certain things are taken away from us (people, places, things, hopes and dreams…). Will Yeshua still be enough? Breathe… keep breathing. Yes, Yeshua is still enough. God is still good. Keep breathing. *Lord, help me to learn what You want me to learn through this pain.* Breathe. Listen to Him. Obey Him. Be patient. Keep breathing. This is progress towards maturity in the Messiah.

> *Beloved friends, if life gets extremely difficult, with many tests, don't be bewildered as though something strange were overwhelming you.*

> *Instead, continue to rejoice, for you, in a measure, have shared in the sufferings of the Anointed One so that you can share in the revelation of his glory and celebrate with even greater gladness!* (1 Peter 4:12-13)

The Silent Treatment

Going through such tests from the Lord has also taught me that He can be *very* quiet during the test. It can almost feel like He is giving us the silent treatment, but we must not mistake His quietness for lack of love. My sister is a teacher, and in the past, she explained something to me about administering tests. She reminded me that teachers cannot talk during tests. They don't want to give the answers away. They want to see how well their students have understood the material.

We can apply these principles to being tested by the Lord, or by Him allowing us to be tested by the devil. The Lord may not say much during the test because He wants to see how well we handle it. At this point, faith in God's character is what we must stand on. Many people in the Bible who were tested (Abraham, Moses, Joseph, and so on) knew their God well. Knowing the Father well is key.

So, during a test, especially when Abba is quiet, we must keep holding onto what we know to be true about the Father, His character, and His promises. My husband and I have found great comfort from the Lord as we reminded ourselves of His goodness, even through tears. Rehearsing Abba's goodness forces us to fix our minds on His true character, instead of our current circumstances.

> Rehearsing Abba's goodness forces us to fix our minds on His true character, instead of our current circumstances.

And never forget that I am with you every day, even to the completion of this age. (Matthew 28:20b)

Entering God's Rest & Letting Go

From personal experience, entering God's rest begins with obedience and pure trust in the Father, even when things don't make sense. This obedience and trust then leads to rest and peace that passes all understanding (especially during trials).

Let us therefore make every effort to enter that rest [of God, to know and experience it for ourselves], so that no one will fall by following the same example of disobedience [as those who died in the wilderness]. (Hebrews 4:11 AMP)

Finally, I have learned that this kind of obedience and trust in Abba forces me to let go of my hold on this life. We should not love our physical life so much that we lose our relationship with Abba by pushing Him away because of grief or loss. Yeshua was a man of sorrows and was also acquainted with grief. Yet this did not stop Him from trusting and obeying His Father in Heaven, and it should not stop us either.

He was despised and rejected by men, a man of deep sorrows who was no stranger to suffering and grief. We hid our faces from him in disgust and considered him a nobody, not worthy of respect. (Isaiah 53:3)

> **We should not love our physical life so much that we lose our relationship with Abba by pushing Him away because of grief or loss.**

Palms-up is the moto the Lord has taught me now. This life is not our own. We are bought with a price. At times, I have seen the Lord use certain tests and trials in my life to pry my hands open until I finally let go of my own agenda – what I wanted, what I really thought I needed. He needed to teach me that He is the one who calls the shots in my life, not me. He is worthy to decide the timing of things regarding my family, my city of residence, friendships, and so on. Not me. It's all up to Him. My life is His. Allowing Abba to navigate my life has finally allowed me to enter my rest in Him, here on earth.

The person who loves his life and pampers himself will miss true life! But the one who detaches his life from this world and abandons himself to me, will find true life and enjoy it forever! (John 12:25)

Have you forgotten that your body is now the sacred temple of the Spirit of Holiness, who lives in you? **You don't belong to yourself any longer**, *for the gift of God, the Holy Spirit, lives inside your sanctuary.*

You were God's expensive purchase, paid for with tears of blood, so by all means, then, use your body to bring glory to God! (1 Corinthians 6:19-20)

Help from Angels

Finally, I must share that the Lord sends angels to minister to us during a test. We can see this in the life of the Messiah. In the desert, Yeshua was tempted by the devil and also dealt with wild animals. However, angels were present also, ministering to His needs. The Amplified translation says they ministered *continually* to Him (Mark 1:13). Angels have assisted me during tests, and I'm sure they are assisting you as well.

Immediately the [Holy] Spirit forced Him out into the wilderness.

He was in the wilderness forty days being tempted [to do evil] by Satan; and He was with the wild animals, and the angels ministered continually to Him. (Mark 1:12-13 AMP)

The day we buried James' precious body was so difficult. That morning, however, before we left the house for the cemetery, our daughter Taylor saw an angel in our front yard. She can see in the Spirit and has witnessed things in the Spirit before. Knowing the Lord sent an angel to help us the morning of such a sorrowful day, highlights how much God loves us and wants us to succeed through these tests.

Are not all the angels ministering spirits sent out [by God] to serve (accompany, protect) those who will inherit salvation? [Of course they are!] (Hebrews 1:14 AMP)

Chapter 4

Led to Spend Time with the Father

Not only was Yeshua baptized by the Holy Spirit and led to be tested, but He was also led to spend time with the Father in prayer. Scripture shows Yeshua getting up early and staying up late to get away with His Heavenly Father. He was with people often, but He also made time to be with the Father. I believe it was this daily time with the Father that fueled His ability to be Spirit led.

> *The next morning, Jesus got up long before daylight, left the house while it was dark, and made his way to a secluded place to give himself to prayer.* (Mark 1:35)

> *After this miracle, the news about Jesus spread even farther. Massive crowds continually gathered to hear him speak and to be healed from their illnesses. But Jesus often slipped away from them and went into the wilderness to pray.* (Luke 5:15-16)

The Book of Genesis clearly demonstrates that from the very beginning, God created man and woman for fellowship. Father God loves spending time with us. Apostle John mentions this fellowship as well.

So we proclaim to you what we have seen and heard about this Life-Giver so that we may share and enjoy this life together. For truly our fellowship is with the Father and with his Son, Jesus, the Anointed One. (1 John 1:3)

Yeshua gave us a beautiful example of how to fellowship with the Father in prayer, daily. Even His disciples saw this fellowship and wanted to know more. They could have asked Yeshua for details on how to heal the sick or how to raise the dead, but that's not what they asked. The disciples asked Yeshua how to pray. They saw this was a key connection between Yeshua and the Father.

One day, as Jesus was in prayer, one of his disciples came over to him as he finished and said, "Would you teach us a model prayer that we can pray, just as John did for his disciples?"

So Jesus taught them this prayer:

"Our heavenly Father, may the glory of your name be the center on which our life turns. May your Holy Spirit come upon us and cleanse us. Manifest your kingdom on earth. And give us our needed bread for the coming day. Forgive our sins as we ourselves release forgiveness to those who have wronged us. And rescue us every time we face tribulations." (Luke 11:1-4)

> **The disciples asked Yeshua how to pray. They saw this was a key connection between Yeshua and the Father.**

Time to Set the Alarm

Over the years, I have realized that consistent time with the Father in prayer is vital. Often, I will get up early to spend time with the Lord because the house is quiet. It's a sacrifice of sleep, but I never regret it. As I seek the Lord first, He always gives me strength for the day.

> *But first and most importantly seek (aim at, strive after)*
> *His kingdom and His righteousness [His way of doing and*
> *being right—the attitude and character of God], and all*
> *these things will be given to you also.* (Matthew 6:33 AMP)

In my quiet time with the Father, I will read His Word and pray. At times, I will also sing to Him in English or in tongues. I will also pray in tongues as I feel led. If you have received the gift of tongues from the Lord (praying in the Spirit), please use it often. Although I do not understand what I am praying, I know the Father does. After using the gift of tongues, I often see answered prayer or other wonderful things manifest in my life and in the lives of those around me.

Time to Set the Alarm

For if I am praying in a tongue, my spirit is engaged in prayer but I have no clear understanding of what is being said.

So here's what I've concluded. I will pray in the Spirit, but I will also pray with my mind engaged. I will sing rapturous praises in the Spirit, but I will also sing with my mind engaged. (1 Corinthians 14:14-15)

As I spend time with the Father consistently this way, not only do things in my life line up with God's will faster, but He also makes quick work of correcting me or guiding me for the day or the near future. He will say things in my heart like,

Be more patient with so-and-so, you don't know what's going on in their life right now.

Stop being jealous of so-and-so. Repent.

Invite so-and-so to the Bible study this week.

I do my best to obey quickly. These nudges from the Father began and have increased after spending much time praying in tongues to the Father. Glory to God.

*Therefore, believers, desire earnestly to prophesy, and **do not forbid speaking in unknown tongues.*** (1 Corinthians 14:39 AMP)

Prayer Helps Us Mature

Consistent prayer time with the Father also produces the fruit of the Spirit within us. Like I mentioned above, not only will the Father guide me and chisel sin out of me during this time, but He will also guide me toward bearing good fruit.

> *But the fruit produced by the Holy Spirit within you is divine love in all its varied expressions: joy that over-flows, peace that subdues, patience that endures, kindness in action, a life full of virtue, faith that prevails, gentle-ness of heart, and strength of spirit. Never set the law above these qualities, for they are meant to be limitless.* (Galatians 5:22-23)

When I sit quietly before the Father and talk and pray with Him about what is hurting in my heart, what I do not understand, or what I need help with, this time allows the Father to make changes in me. This process matures me. He washes over me with Bible verses, or speaks to me in His still, small voice. Sometimes, He will use impressions or stories from Scripture to guide me with His answer. Sometimes He answers right then, but not always. It can take a day or two, or some-times longer, but He always answers my heart's cry and helps me as I seek Him and spend time with Him. When clarity or the answers come, I thank Him and make the changes needed, and continue to mature day by day.

Sadly, the flip side can also be true. If I do *not* take the time to spend with Abba daily or often, and consistently sleep in or misuse my time, I do not grow much in the Lord that week. I see myself floundering with the same concepts or unanswered questions again and again because I have not taken time to be with the Father, alone. Fellowship with the Father is a choice. He is always ready to spend time with us. Do we want to spend time with Him? (I am speaking to myself as well). I hope we are all saying, *"Yes!"*

> Fellowship with Abba is a choice. He is always ready to spend time with us. Do we want to spend time with Him?

'For I know the plans and thoughts that I have for you,' says the Lord, 'plans for peace and well-being and not for disaster, to give you a future and a hope.

Then you will call on Me and you will come and pray to Me, and I will hear [your voice] and I will listen to you.

*Then [with a deep longing] you will seek Me and require Me [as a vital necessity] and **[you will] find Me when you search for Me with all your heart.'** (Jeremiah 29:11-13 AMP)

Chapter 5

Led in Big Decisions

Being led by the Holy Spirit is very helpful in many ways, but some of you may be wondering how practical all of this is. Can the Holy Spirit guide us with making big decisions in life as well?

Does the Lord care about my job or who I work for? Would He guide me with who to marry? Does He care about where I live?

Well… there are no Bible verses that say:

"Thou shalt live here and not there." or *"Thou shalt marry so-and-so."*

But that is where the Holy Spirit comes in and leads us each individually. The Father will absolutely guide us with these big decisions if we have ears to hear. In fact, He set the boundaries of when and where we will live on earth, and even knows the smallest details of our lives.

> He will absolutely guide us with these big decisions if we have ears to hear.

From one man, Adam, he made every man and woman and every race of humanity, and he spread us over all the earth. He sets the boundaries of people and nations, determining their appointed times in history. He has done this so that every person would long for God, feel their way to him, and find him—for he is the God who is easy to discover! (Acts 17:26-27)

Are not five sparrows sold for two copper coins? Yet not one of them has been forgotten in the presence of God. Indeed the very hairs of your head are all numbered. Do not be afraid; you are far more valuable than many sparrows. (Luke 12:6-7 AMP)

So, if the Lord knows the number of hairs on our head, believe me... He also knows where He wants us to work and to live. He can get this information over to us if we are willing to listen and to be led by Him.

Time to Tune into the Spirit

Earlier in my walk with the Lord, I used to rush through making big decisions. Time after time however, I noticed certain jobs and relationships would not work out because I hadn't sought the Lord very well or hadn't waited on Him for answers. Over the years however, I have learned to slow down and pray about big decisions. My husband and I often cover big decisions in prayer *together*. If you have someone in your life who also loves the Lord, please ask them to join you in prayer during these big decisions.

In Scripture, we see that Yeshua sought His Father regarding a very big decision. He was about to appoint His apostles, but beforehand, He spent time in prayer with His Father.

After leaving the synagogue, Jesus went into the high hills
to spend the whole night in prayer to God. At daybreak,
he called together all of his followers and selected twelve
from among them, and he appointed them to be his apos-
tles. (Luke 6:12-13)

In addition to praying and spending time with the Father regarding big decisions, sometimes we must wait for His answer. Patience is hard, but it is a fruit of the Spirit, and one that all mature believers in Yeshua must have (Galatians 5:22-23).

After seeking the Lord about a big decision, we must wait on Him until we get a clear answer. It may take days, weeks, months, or even longer. Waiting on Abba can be *very* challenging, but the Lord's wisdom is worth waiting for. My husband and I often notice that as the time draws closer to making a big decision, the Holy Spirit will drop a nugget of guidance into our hearts. At times this has been a dream, a word of wisdom, an impression from the Holy Spirit, or something similar. But it is something obvious that we cannot make up or pass off as a coincidence. Sometimes the confirmation even comes in doubles – two signs within a day or two or a double dream regarding what we should do. We love it when this happens, knowing we have received the Lord's answer clearly regarding the big decision.

And if anyone longs to be wise, ask God for wisdom and he
will give it! He won't see your lack of wisdom as an oppor-
tunity to scold you over your failures but he will over-
whelm your failures with his generous grace. (James 1:5)

Apostle Paul and a Man from Macedonia

In the Book of Acts, we see Apostle Paul being led by the Holy Spirit to make some big decisions. During one of his missionary journeys, Paul was deciding where to go next to preach the gospel. He attempted to go various places, but the Holy Spirit redirected him. He obeyed the leading of the Holy Spirit and was successful because of it.

> *The Holy Spirit had forbidden Paul and his partners to preach the word in the southwestern provinces of Turkey, so they ministered throughout the region of central and west-central Turkey.*

> *When they got as far west as the borders of Mysia, they repeatedly attempted to go north into the province of Bithynia, but again the Spirit of Yeshua would not allow them to enter. So instead they went right on through the province of Mysia to the seaport of Troas.*

> *While staying there Paul experienced a supernatural, ecstatic vision during the night. A man from Macedonia appeared before him, pleading with him, "You must come across the sea to Macedonia and help us!"*

> *After Paul had this vision, we immediately prepared to cross over to Macedonia, convinced that God himself was calling us to go and preach the wonderful news of the gospel to them.* (Acts 16:6-10)

This passage demonstrates the various styles Holy Spirit can use to lead us: dreams, visions, opens doors, shuts doors, and so on. The key is in the waiting. Time and time again, the answers from Holy Spirit have come in the eleventh hour. As we waited on the Holy Spirit, these daunting, big decisions suddenly became bite size pieces. The first bite was the first thing Holy Spirit confirmed or showed us to do. He does not often show the entire ball field with flood lights. It's more of a lamp-to-our-feet experience. It seems He is watching our faith. Once we obey the first thing He tells us to do, He will send another step or sign for us to obey. If we obey, He will send another step and another. Step by step, He has led us successfully through many big decisions.

> **The key is in the waiting. Time and time again, the answers from Holy Spirit have come in the eleventh hour.**

Your word is a lamp to my feet and a light to my path.
(Psalm 119:105 NKJV)

Goodbye California

Back in January of 2021 when covid enforcements were really picking up, Sam's boss (Mr. Biden) asked all federal employees to get the covid shot. As we prayed about it, there was no peace in our hearts for Sam to take the shot – even if it cost him his job. He applied for a religious exemption, but the human resource department did not respond. As the date drew closer for Sam to show the FAA (Federal Aviation

Administration) the evidence of his compliance, we began to seek the Lord heavily for direction.

Sam's job was our main source of income, so we kept praying and praying for wisdom. Finally, in the eleventh hour when the date to show compliance was almost upon us, the Holy Spirit dropped an extremely clear word into my heart to sell our home. We didn't know where God wanted us to go. He said nothing about that yet, but it was very clear He wanted us to sell our home. Shortly after deciding to obey and sell our home, two separate individuals at our church had words of wisdom from the Lord about us leaving California and quickly. These words of wisdom totally confirmed what Holy Spirit had already been telling us. Then, just to be *super* clear and awesome, a couple days later, the Lord confirmed His desire for us to leave California by way of a prophetic dream.

So, we obeyed quickly. We put our home on the market and began packing our bags, even though we *still* didn't know where we were going! As we drove east, the realtor called and told us we had an offer on our home. Abba allowed the sale to go through quickly, which was a huge blessing. By faith, Sam decided to leave the FAA, and not long afterward God provided another job for him that did not require the shot. The Lord also provided a home for us to live in over in North Carolina. Although this was a *huge* decision for us, the Holy Spirit led us every step of the way. All glory to God!

If you are hard pressed with a big decision, make sure to ask the Father for wisdom, wait on Him for guidance, then obey quickly when He directs you.

> *Don't be pulled in different directions or worried about*
> *a thing. Be saturated in prayer throughout each day,*

offering your faith-filled requests before God with over-flowing gratitude. Tell him every detail of your life, then God's wonderful peace that transcends human understanding, will guard your heart and mind through Jesus Christ. (Philippians 4:6-7)

Chapter 6

Led Every Day

T o some, being led by the Holy Spirit in big decisions makes sense, but what about the little things in life – the daily happenings. Is it possible to be led by the Holy Spirit every day? Let's look at Yeshua's life for the answer. Was He led daily, even in the small things? Well, He often spoke of being led by the Father to do and to say certain things throughout His day. This sounds like immense self-control and maturity, but it also sounds like being led daily! And we know if the Father and the Spirit led Yeshua daily, They can lead us daily as well, *if we are willing.*

> *So Jesus said, I speak to you eternal truth. The Son is unable to do anything from himself or through his own initiative. I only do the works that I see the Father doing, for the Son does the same works as his Father.* (John 5:19)

> *For I'm not speaking as someone who is self-appointed, but I speak by the authority of the Father himself who sent me, and who instructed me what to say. And I know that the Father's commands result in eternal life, and*

that's why I speak the very words I've heard him speak.
(John 12:49-50)

Philip and the Ethiopian

As another example of being led daily, let's look at Philip's story in Scripture (Acts 8). Philip had been preaching the gospel in Samaria for a while. One day, the Angel of the Lord told him to go from Jerusalem down to Gaza by way of a desert road. Philip didn't ask questions or delay. He obeyed without hesitation. As he traveled along the desert road, the Holy Spirit led him to come alongside an Ethiopian who was also traveling on the same road. After Philip shared the gospel with the Ethiopian, the man accepted Yeshua as his Savior and was baptized in water shortly afterward. This is a beautiful story of how our daily *yes* to being led by the Holy Spirit can impact the Kingdom of Heaven.

If you noticed, it was *after* Philip's obedience to travel the desert road that the Holy Spirit showed him the next step (to go up to the Ethiopian). The Lord did not explain everything in advance. In Scripture and in my own life, the Holy Spirit seems to provide guidance one step at a time. Will we humbly obey with child-like faith, even if we don't understand?

> In Scripture and in my own life, the Holy Spirit seems to provide guidance one step at a time.

The Holy Spirit said to Philip, "Go and walk alongside the chariot." So Philip ran to catch up. (Acts 8:29-30a)

Jesus called a little one to his side and said to them,

"Learn this well: Unless you dramatically change your way of thinking and become teachable like a little child, you will never be able to enter in. Whoever continually humbles himself to become like this little child is the greatest one in heaven's kingdom realm." (Matthew 18:2-4)

Isn't God too Busy for the Small Stuff?

Early in our marriage, I remember Sam asking me this very question. Sam was a new believer in the Lord, and didn't want to bother God with small things that were going on in his life. If Sam needed help with something small, maybe something at work or with a co-worker, I would ask him if he prayed about it. Sam would usually respond with something like,

"Babe, God doesn't care about small things like my day at work. I really don't want to bother Him with it. He has enough on His plate with wars, famines, and other world problems."

Here and there, I continued mentioning how much God cares for us, even in the small things. Something must've clicked for Sam, because a year or two later he started asking God for help at work and began coming home with almost daily testimonies of answered prayer. Praise Adonai! He really does care about the small stuff. The Father is never too busy for us or for what is going on in our lives.

A Shortcut if You Are Open to It

Like I mentioned in an earlier chapter, hearing the Lord's voice more clearly, really began for me after I increased my time with praying in tongues. As I began to pray in tongues almost daily and for longer periods of time, something amazing shifted in the Spirit. During my prayer time in English then, I began to hear the Father speak into my heart. He would ask a question and I would answer. It became a beautiful, rolling conversation.

> **Hearing the Lord's voice more clearly, really began for me after I increased my time with praying in tongues.**

The correspondence continued outside my prayer time as well. While I gardened, He would talk with me in my heart about the garden and give me spiritual lessons or remind me of parables or passages from the Bible. While I was on a walk, He would drop revelation into my heart about something I had asked the day before. We were finally connected in a beautiful, fluid manner unlike I had ever known.

> *The one who speaks in tongues advances his own spiritual progress, while the one who prophesies builds up the church.* (1 Corinthians 14:4)

Please do not be discouraged if you have not received the gift of tongues. Remember, the Holy Spirit decides who gets what gift. But I *would* recommend asking the Father for it, and let Him decide.

Not everyone is an apostle or a prophet or a teacher. Not everyone performs miracles or has gifts of healing or speaks in tongues or interprets tongues. (1 Corinthians 12:29-30)

In the meantime, keep using whatever gift(s) you have been given by the Holy Spirit, as He leads you. Keep spending time with Abba in prayer and in His Word. You *will* learn to hear His voice. Then just keep following His voice, nudges, and impressions throughout the day.

Morning Walk and a School Bus

About a year ago, I was out for my morning walk. As I came to the end of our street, there was a school bus picking up children. Rounding the corner, I passed a father standing outside his home, watching his child or children getting onto the bus. In those moments, I sensed this man was a good father. Continuing a few paces, the impression sank deep within my soul as the Holy Spirit said in my heart:

That man is a good father.

Then I sensed in my spirit,

Turn around and tell him, quickly.

Instantly, my mind was full of excuses,

Lord, I don't know this man. What if it's just me talking? What if…

But then in a fraction of a second, somehow I understood I had three more steps to make my decision before he went back inside his home. Not wanting to regret missing this opportunity, and knowing the Lord would embolden me, I turned around to obey.

Walking up to the man, I mustered all the calmness in my voice that I could and shyly began,

"Excuse me Sir, I love the Lord very much. As I walked by you just now, I believe the Lord gave me a message for you."

Morning Walk and a School Bus

His eyes opened wide,

"Really?" he said, attentively.

Nervous, but courage growing within me, I continued,

"Yes, as I walked by you just now, I heard the Holy Spirit say that you are a good father."

Nothing could have prepared me for what happened next. An expression of immense relief flooded this man's face as he said,

"You have no idea how much this means to me. It's been so tough lately with these kiddos (as he pointed to the bus). I really needed this encouragement today. My wife and I love the Lord, but it's just been tough lately. I've heard about things like this at church – is this how it works?"

I'm sure I said *yes*, and then we spoke about his family and mine for a little while. Then I continued on my walk.

I am still learning, but regarding words of wisdom and words of knowledge and how they work, this man was correct. They are fairly simple. Someone senses a word or phrase or even an impression from the Lord. They obey and share it, and the person is blessed. It is important to note the Holy Spirit can operate outside the church as well. He can ask us to minister anywhere, anytime. That is why we must be ready to listen and obey His voice daily. In this way, we will never miss an opportunity to advance the Kingdom of Heaven.

So, what started out as a routine morning walk, ended up being a divine appointment led by the Holy Spirit. This man needed a hug from the Lord and what a blessing to be part of it. All glory to God.

> *Take advantage of every opportunity to be a blessing to others, especially to our brothers and sisters in the family of faith!* (Galatians 6:10)

Eaves-Dropping at the Gorilla Exhibit

Here is another example of how the Lord can lead us in the little, daily things. Sam and I have been homeschooling our children for years. Now and then, I will look for fun adventures outside the home to mix up the book learning with hands-on-learning. One spring afternoon, I had taken the kids on a field trip to our local zoo. As we walked along, enjoying the giraffes, elephants, and so on, my guard was down (spiritually). We were all having such a great time being outside, enjoying God's creation, and admiring all the animals. Then it happened: I overheard some moms talking behind us as we were all filing into a narrow path to see the gorillas.

I overheard one mom speaking to another,

"You know all the things the kids are coming home with from school these days, I'm just not ready for it. I mean, we talk it through and discuss what Jesus thinks about each topic, but there is just so much going on!"

In those moments, I wondered to myself if that mom had considered homeschooling her kiddos. A couple steps later, the Holy Spirit said deep inside my spirit,

Have you considered homeschool?

The impression was,

I want you to ask her this exact question.

In all honesty, I'm ashamed to say that I debated with the Lord a bit as we kept walking, thinking to myself,

This is my day off. I'm on a field trip, Lord. Can I please just relax today and enjoy the animals and my kids? (I know – shame on me!)

Then the Spirit gave me courage and love for this mom. Realizing my selfishness and that I was bought at a price, I humbled myself.

Lord, if that was You speaking just now in my heart, bring us together at the gorilla exhibit up ahead. I'll ask her.

Sure enough, she parked her stroller near us and the courage just flowed from Holy Spirit. Walking up to her, I began with something like,

"Hi, I love Yeshua very much, and couldn't help but overhear your conversation with your mom-friend about the school and all the things the kids are coming home with. As I overheard you, I believe Holy Spirit asked me to come to you. He wants to know if you have considered homeschool?"

Her attentive, sweet face turned into an excited smile as she said,

"You know what, yes! I have considered it (pointing to her two mom-friends). They both homeschool and they have been asking me about it as well, I just don't think I am smart enough to teach my kids. Do you homeschool?"

Smiling, I gathered my kiddos around me and answered,

"Yes, I homeschool them all, and you absolutely can homeschool your kids as well. If God is calling you to homeschool, He will give you everything you need, step by step. You will be an amazing teacher for your children."

A look of relief and excitement came over her face. We spoke a little longer and then we left the exhibit. Perhaps that was the tipping point for her – for a perfect stranger to encourage her from the Lord to consider homeschool. Whatever the reason, I was happy to be used for God's glory.

Have you forgotten that your body is now the sacred temple of the Spirit of Holiness, who lives in you? You don't belong to yourself any longer, for the gift of God, the Holy Spirit, lives inside your sanctuary.

You were God's expensive purchase, paid for with tears of blood, so by all means, then, use your body to bring glory to God! (1 Corinthians 6:19-20)

The Key is Obedience

I share these stories not to brag, but to give God all the glory and demonstrate that being led by the Holy Spirit daily is quite simple. It just requires obedience. Often, the Lord bakes these nudges to help someone right into my day. It's so fulfilling and exciting too!

I just want to obey all you ask of me. So teach me, Lord, for you are my God. Your gracious Spirit is all I need, so lead me on good paths that are pleasing to you, my one and only God! (Psalm 143:10)

Chapter 7

Led When We Don't Feel Qualified

H as the Lord ever asked you to do something big for Him that surprised you? Or has He ever flashed something to you in a prophetic dream that you *never* thought possible? If you are not familiar with prophetic dreams, don't worry. We will discuss them in a later chapter. But over the years, I've noticed the Lord is far more interested in my *yes*, than my current qualifications or capabilities. So, when Abba gives us an impression of doing something *way* beyond our wheelhouse, may we all say yes by faith, and allow Him to work out all the "impossible" details along the way.

> Over the years, I've noticed the Lord is far more interested in my yes, than my current qualifications or capabilities.

Brothers and sisters, consider who you were when God called you to salvation. Not many of you were wise scholars by human standards, nor were many of you in positions of power. Not many of you were considered the elite when you answered God's call.

But God chose those whom the world considers foolish to shame those who think they are wise, and God chose the puny and powerless to shame the high and mighty. (1 Corinthians 1:26-27)

Gideon and the Angel of the Lord

Some of you may have heard this story before, but it highlights how Abba uses the humble people of this world to do great things. You can read the entire story of Gideon in Judges 6-8. In summary, the Israelites were living in the land of promise, but had not been obeying the Lord. Therefore, their land was overrun with Midianites who were oppressing them like crazy, destroying their crops, and leaving them with no livestock. Because of this, the Israelites cried out to the Lord. Finally, one day, the Angel of the Lord came to visit Gideon and asked him to do something *way* outside of his comfort zone. Let's listen in on their conversation.

> *Yahweh's Angel suddenly appeared to Gideon and said, "Yahweh's presence goes with you, man of fearless courage!"*

> *"Me?" Gideon replied. "But sir, if Yahweh is truly with us, why have all these troubles come to us? Where are all his miracle-wonders that our fathers told us about when they said, 'Did not Yahweh deliver us out of Egypt?' But now Yahweh has abandoned us and put us under the power of the Midianites."*

Then Yahweh himself faced Gideon directly and said, "Am I not sending you? With my presence you have all you need. Go in the strength that you now have and rescue Israel from Midian's power!"

Gideon said to him, "But Lord, how could I ever rescue Israel? Of all the thousands in Manasseh, my clan is the weakest, and I'm the least qualified in my family."

Yahweh replied, "My presence and my power will be with you. Believe me, Gideon, you will crush the Midianites as easily as if they were only one man!" (Judges 6:12-16)

The Lord indeed kept His Word and brought about a mighty victory for Gideon and his small army of three hundred men. In turn, this victory broke off the oppression of the Midianites and gave Israel peace for a time. In the end, it wasn't about how qualified Gideon felt, or what tribe he was from. It was about his obedience to the Lord. He gave God his yes and God took care of the rest. Hallelujah!

Becoming an Author

About three years ago, after my husband and I experienced our third miscarriage in a row, I was extremely discouraged. I told the Father that if He would help us learn how to overcome these miscarriages and have more children, that I would testify to others about it and give Him all the glory. About that time, we had also experienced an immense healing miracle for our daughter, Julia that we had been praying for and believing for, for about a year and a half. Praise Adonai!

The Father took me up on my offer to testify right away, and encouraged me to write a book about our lives. He encouraged me to be thorough, sharing both the pain and the joy of what it means to walk with our Lord and Savior and how He is always faithful. Wanting to obey, but not quite sure how to begin, or even if I was author material, my thoughts rambled in my head.

How do I write about our lives, Lord? I'm just a stay-at-home mom...In the past, You've helped me teach Sunday school and I do love homeschooling the kids, but a book audience would be mostly adults, right? That's intimidating to me, Lord. Are You sure? This seems so impossible!

But still wanting to obey, I agreed.

"Alright Abba.... but where do I start?"

His answer was more of an impression inside my heart.

Open Word document and start at the beginning (of your story).

So practical... so easy. As I began to write each chapter from my heart, the thoughts, concepts, and Bible verses began to flow. The Lord guided me every step of the way. As the pages began to fill, I paused now and then while our lives took several hard left-hand turns, and even what seemed a U-turn — the loss of James almost full-term. It took time for me to process these things emotionally, and time to ask Abba questions about these things. But by God's grace, He helped me continue to learn and grow, and I kept filling the chapters with the concepts He was teaching me. Through faith in the Lord, often in tears, I kept writing, believing Abba would help me finish the book.

When I felt the book was almost ready for publishing, the Lord led me to a new friend in North Carolina who had already self-published a book and understood the process. Meeting her was pivotal, and absolutely designed by God. She explained what publishing company she used and how the process of self-publishing worked. This was the path God had designed for me and His timing was perfect (as usual). He literally walked me right into what He asked me to do, even though originally it seemed impossible. He provided everything and everyone I needed to write and publish the book. All glory to God!

> *For we are His workmanship, created in Jesus Christ for good works, which God prepared beforehand that we should walk in them.* (Ephesians 2:10 NKJV)

The book is now published. It is called *A Friend of God – Through Sorrow and Grief, Joy and Laughter*. I pray many are blessed by it. I realize now that it was never about how I felt or if I was qualified to write… it was only about my *yes*, and God took care of the rest.

> **Then Mary responded, saying, "Yes!** *I will be a mother for the Lord! As his servant, I accept whatever he has for me. May everything you have told me come to pass." And the angel left her.* (Luke 1:38)

Shavuot and My Freewill Offering

Shavuot is what the church normally calls Pentecost Sunday or Feast of Weeks. Over the past five years or so, the Lord has been gently guiding me and my family to revisit His commandments in Scripture and to obey them. One of them is His command to celebrate His annual Festivals – *forever*. There are seven of them, and they represent His first and second coming to earth. During the Feast of Weeks (Shavuot), we are encouraged in the Book of Deuteronomy to give a freewill offering to the Lord like the priests used to do when they would wave the loaves of bread before the Lord.

"You shall count seven weeks for yourself; you shall begin to count seven weeks from the time you first put the sickle to the standing grain.

Then you shall celebrate the Feast of Weeks to the Lord your God with a tribute of a freewill offering from your hand, which you shall give [to Him] just as the Lord your God blesses you;" (Deuteronomy 16:9-10 AMP)

As Feast of Weeks was coming closer, I asked the Lord quietly in my heart,

Abba, what would You like from me for the Feast of Weeks? I want to give You a freewill offering from my hand. You've given me so much! What would You like from me? What can I bless You with... I know You have everything... but still...

The Lord responded quickly in my heart,

Record and share the two songs I have given you.

Excited but overwhelmed, my heart about skipped a beat. I had never recorded songs before. How *in the world* would I accomplish this? The songs were heart-gripping, about continuing to live for the Lord and even to worship Him through suffering. He gave them to me as a gift of comfort to encourage me as we coped with the loss of James as well as other miscarriages we'd experienced. Tears flooded my eyes often as I sang these songs to the Lord. Singing them kept healing my heart little by little on a very deep level.

After receiving this Word from the Lord to record and share these songs, I began to increase my practice time and prayed about when and how to share them with others. Months before receiving these beautiful songs from the Lord, Abba had allowed me to meet an amazing mom-friend through a local church. She plays the piano and sings beautifully for the Lord, and had mentioned a recording studio down town that she had used in the past. Remembering this, I reached out to her and asked for details. She was happy to help.

I felt led to book a recording session as soon as possible with this local studio. In addition, about three days prior to recording, the Lord provided the money to cover the studio fee! Every time I turned around, Abba was outdoing Himself. I had nothing to fear. I had nothing to worry about.

What initially sounded like an overwhelming request from the Lord, was not at all. He provided the friend who knew all about the recording studio, He covered the recording fees, and He even guided me how to upload the songs with videos and pictures in the background (something new to me as well). Right before I uploaded them, I prayed over them and gave them to Abba as my free will offering in honor of His Feast of Weeks.

Both songs are available now if you'd like to listen. YouTube Channel: *HomeschoolingForHisKingdom*. I pray many are blessed and encouraged by them.

"Run Your Race" and *"You are Worthy of My Praise"*

Many people have reached out, explaining how they were moved to tears by the weight of the first song, and how powerful the second song is as well. All glory to God! Again, it wasn't about whether I felt qualified to record these songs or if I already knew how to or not. These songs are from Abba and He was simply looking for my *yes*. He helped me with the rest. Praise Adonai!

> *And God is able to make all grace abound toward you, that you, always having all sufficiency in all things, may have an abundance for every good work.* (2 Corinthians 9:8 NKJV)

Chapter 8

Led to Use Our Gifts & Talents

Has anyone every told you that the Lord wrote a book about you? From what I can see in Scripture, He made a book about each one of us. These books seem to include what He wants us to accomplish on earth for His Kingdom.

> *You saw who you created me to be before I became me!*
> *Before I'd ever seen the light of day, the number of days*
> *you planned for me were already recorded in your book.*
> (Psalm 139:16)

It appears that one day, the followers of the Messiah will be judged by the Lord – *from these books*. Abba will look at what He wrote about us in our book vs. what we actually did while on earth.

> *And I saw a great white throne and Him who was seated*
> *upon it, from whose presence earth and heaven fled away,*
> *and no place was found for them [for this heaven and*
> *earth are passing away].*

And I saw the dead, the great and the small, standing before the throne, and books were opened. Then another book was opened, which is the Book of Life; **and the dead were judged according to what they had done as written in the books** *[that is, everything done while on earth].* (Revelation 20:11-12 AMP)

Being audited by the Lord someday should be concerning to all of us. The Father invested in each one of us immensely with Yeshua's death on the cross. Should He not rightly expect something in return from us? Yes, He should. The Scriptures are full of passages reminding us that we were bought at a price, that this life is not our own, that He will prune us, that we must bear fruit, and so on.

I am the true Vine, and My Father is the vinedresser. Every branch in Me that does not bear fruit, He takes away; and every branch that continues to bear fruit, He [repeatedly] prunes, so that it will bear more fruit [even richer and finer fruit]. (John 15:1-2 AMP)

My Father is glorified and honored by this, when you bear much fruit, and prove yourselves to be My [true] disciples. (John 15:8 AMP)

Not only is this life not our own, but Abba has also deposited many gifts and talents inside of us. He expects us to use these gifts and talents for His Kingdom. Matthew 25:14-30 contains a parable about Abba's investment in us. In summary, a master of three servants gave each one of them gold according to the master's opinion of how much they could manage while he was away. When he returned, the first two servants did well and gave him a wonderful return because they invested what he had given them wisely. However, the third servant did not. He was nervous about losing the master's money, so he did not invest it at all. This servant provided nothing in return for the master. This made the master very angry, so he gave the gold from the third servant to the first. Then he called the third servant wicked and had him thrown into outer darkness.

> *For to everyone who has [and values his blessings and gifts from God, and has used them wisely], more will be given, and [he will be richly supplied so that] he will have an abundance; but from the one who does not have [because he has ignored or disregarded his blessings and gifts from God], even what he does have will be taken away.*
>
> *And throw out the worthless servant into the outer darkness; in that place [of grief and torment] there will be weeping [over sorrow and pain] and grinding of teeth [over distress and anger].* (Matthew 25:29-30 AMP)

Yikes! This sounds very serious, and it truly is. Similar to how the master gave his servants gold and left for a time, the Father has given each one of us gifts and talents and has gone away for a time. He will return to us like the master returned in the parable. When He does, He will expect an accounting from us based on what He has given us.

Gifts and Talents

Let's break down some of these gifts and talents the Father has given us. What are they, and where do we find them in Scripture? The whole chapter of 1 Corinthians 12 is helpful regarding this topic, but let's look at several key verses.

4 It is the same Holy Spirit who continues to distribute many different varieties of gifts. 5 The Lord Yahweh is one, and he is the one who apportions to believers different varieties of ministries.

6 The same God distributes different kinds of miracles that accomplish different results through each believer's gift and ministry as he energizes and activates them.

7 Each believer is given continuous revelation by the Holy Spirit to benefit not just himself but all. 8 For example: The Spirit gives to one the gift of the word of wisdom. To another, the same Spirit gives the gift of the word of revelation knowledge.

9 And to another, the same Spirit gives the gift of faith. And to another, the same Spirit gives gifts of healing.

10 And to another the power to work miracles. And to another the gift of prophecy. And to another the gift to discern what the Spirit is speaking. And to another the gift of speaking different kinds of tongues. And to another the gift of interpretation of tongues.

11 Remember, it is the same Holy Spirit who distributes, activates, and operates these different gifts as he chooses for each believer. (1 Corinthians 12:4-11)

Romans 12:6-8 talks about additional gifts like encouragement, serving, and meeting people's needs. Ephesians 4 describes other gifts as well, like teaching, evangelizing, and so on. There are so many gifts and talents the Lord can give to the believer. Some of you may already know what yours are, others may not. If some of you are unsure of what your gifts and talents from the Lord may be, please ask a close friend or relative or the Holy Spirit Himself. Once you realize what you are naturally good at and what brings you excitement or joy in the Lord, lean into it. That skill is most likely a God-given talent which the Lord needs you to use for His Kingdom. Then ask the Holy Spirit to lead you (or continue leading you) in these giftings and talents.

At times Abba uses the gifts He has given me to minister to non-believers, but He most often uses them through me to encourage other believers.

*For his "body" has been formed in his image and is closely joined together and constantly connected as one. And every member has been given divine gifts to contribute to the growth of all; **and as these gifts operate effectively throughout the whole body, we are built up and made perfect in love.*** (Ephesians 4:16)

Fresh Water Springs and a Gatorade

About a month ago, for the first time *ever*, my family and I went to swim in a fresh water spring here in Florida. Many of our local friends told us how beautiful and clear these springs were. Full of anticipation, we set out with swim suits, towels, and goggles.

It was a very hot, sunny day in Florida (about 100 degrees). We pulled into the state park, and Sam drove up behind the last vehicle waiting to enter. As we slowly made our way to the front of the line of cars, my eyes drifted to a young teen directing traffic up ahead. Her cheeks were flushed, and she was sweating.

Fresh Water Springs and a Gatorade

The Holy Spirit instantly gave me the impression of giving her a Gatorade. I mentioned it to Sam, but the drinks were in the back of the van in the cooler. Unable to shake the nudge, I prayed quickly that if I had heard correctly, that someone would give her something to drink or help her in some way.

We had a refreshing time at the springs, and *yes,* the water certainly was clear! We were all packed up in the van and were ready to head home. As we rounded the corner to leave the park, my eyes fell on that same sweet girl again, still directing traffic at the entrance/exit. This time, sweat was all over her face – she was bright red. Bless her. The same impression lit up my spirit, this time 100-fold,

"Sam – let's give her a Gatorade!"

Sam, having just brought up several Gatorades from the cooler before we took off, was already preparing to roll down his window and give her one. I'm sure Holy Spirit was speaking to him too and probably even had him prepare by grabbing a bunch right before we left the park.

As Sam rolled down the window and offered her a Gatorade, she brimmed with a relieved smile saying,

"Thank you so much – you have no idea! You have no idea!"

As we slowly rolled away, we saw in the review mirror that she immediately opened the Gatorade and was chugging it. That poor girl! Bless her. Maybe she forgot to bring her water that day, or maybe she wasn't allowed a break in a while. Like she said, *we had no idea.* I wish we obeyed His nudge on our way in, but by God's grace, He allowed us to still obey on our way out. That day the Father gave me a word of knowledge (an impression), another day it may be something else. Whatever gift or talent the Holy Spirit wants to use within us, may we be willing and obedient.

As I obey the Spirit's leading, He usually guides me with the next thing I am to do or to say (if any). I just keep flowing with His guidance until the interaction is finished. Sometimes I get nervous, but the more I obey, the easier it is to trust Him. He knows what He is doing and wants to love people through us if we allow Him to. Our obedience to His guidance is key.

> *For example: The Spirit gives to one the gift of the word of wisdom. To another, the same Spirit gives the gift of the word of revelation knowledge. And to another, the same Spirit gives the gift of faith. And to another, the same Spirit gives gifts of healing.* (1 Corinthians 12:8-9)

Tongues with Interpretation on a Walk

About two years ago, as I was on my usual walk, I began to pray for a certain friend of mine. Feeling led, I began to pray in tongues for her, then English prayers, then more tongues. That day, I asked for the interpretation of what I was praying in tongues. The Father answered quickly with something like,

She needs to stop being afraid. Tell her to repent of fear.

Concerned for my friend, but also concerned I may have gotten it wrong, I'm sure I asked a couple more times for confirmation, but the message or feeling in my heart did not change. When I got back from my walk, by faith I text my friend a simple message of how I had been praying for her in tongues and also in English. I explained it seemed the interpretation of tongues was for her to repent of fear. He didn't tell me about what, and I didn't ask. I simply relayed what I heard, trying not to add or take away from anything He said.

> *So then, if you speak in a tongue, pray for the interpretation to be able to unfold the meaning of what you are saying.* (1 Corinthians 14:13)

After not hearing back from her for a day or two, my heart began to sink,

Man, I must've missed it. Haven't heard from my good friend in almost two days now. She's probably reconsidering our friendship, she's probably...

And then she text me. I was blown away at how accurate the Spirit of the Lord was. Her reply was something like this,

"Katie, I prayed about your text when I received it. At the time, I didn't realize I had fear in my heart about such-and-such. It was underlying and hidden. The Spirit revealed it, and I repented. Thank you for praying for me and for stepping out in faith with your message. Love you."

I was astonished, relieved, and so thankful Abba helped me obey. I use this example of tongues with interpretation to give God the glory, but also to show you how using your gifts and talents for the Lord is often crucial to building up the body of the Lord. Even if you don't know the details, the Spirit does. If He trusts you with a straight word like this for someone whether from tongues with interpretation, word of wisdom, or a prophecy, please be obedient. And be careful not to add to what you heard or take away from it either. Let the chips fall where they may. You are the messenger.

In those moments prior to pressing "send" on my phone, I had to be more concerned about my obedience to the Father than whether my good friend would remain my good friend. Remember, these gifts are not for us to use when we feel like it. We are to use them when we are led by the Spirit. We will all give an account some day for what we did with what we were given. May we all be good stewards with the gifts and talents the Lord has given us.

> I had to be more concerned about my obedience to the Father than whether my good friend would remain my good friend.

Therefore, each one must answer for himself and give a personal account of his own life before God. (Romans 14:12)

Chapter 9

Led to Love and Help Others

One thing Yeshua emphasized while He was on earth, was how much He wanted us to love others. Some people are easier to love than others, but they are all made in God's image. The Father asks us to not hate or bear a grudge against our brother or neighbor, but actually to love them like we love ourselves.

> *You shall not hate your brother in your heart; you may most certainly rebuke your neighbor, but shall not incur sin because of him.*
>
> *You shall not take revenge nor bear any grudge against the sons of your people, but you shall love your neighbor (acquaintance, associate, companion) as yourself; I am the Lord.* (Leviticus 19:17-18)

One day when Yeshua was being quizzed by a religious scholar regarding which commandment in the Law is the most important, He answered by quoting from Leviticus 19 and Deuteronomy 6.

You are to love the Lord Yahweh, your God, with a passionate heart, from the depths of your soul, with your every thought, and with all your strength. This is the great and supreme commandment. And the second is this: **You must love your neighbor in the same way you love yourself.** *You will never find a greater commandment than these.* (Mark 12:30-31)

Many years before Yeshua even walked the earth, Abba Father made it very clear in the last six of the ten commandments that we are to love others and treat them well (Exodus 20). In fact, God's emphasis on loving others goes back even further than Moses and the ten commandments to Cain right outside the Garden of Eden. God's conversation with Cain shows us how much He values human life. The consequences that Cain had to bear from murdering his brother Abel, instead of loving him, were extremely harsh (Genesis 4:1-16). The Lord loves everyone, and He desires for us to love them too.

If anyone says, "I love God," and hates (works against) his brother he is a liar; for the one who does not love his brother whom he has seen, cannot love God whom he has not seen. And this commandment we have from Him, that the one who loves God should also [unselfishly] love his brother and seek the best for him. (1 John 4:20-21 AMP)

As we are being led by the Holy Spirit, we should not be surprised when the leading is for someone else, and has nothing to do with ourselves. Remember, as followers of Yeshua we were bought at a price.

Yeshua gave His life for us. We must be willing to be used by the Lord to love others.

> **The Lord loves everyone, and He
> desires for us to love them too.**

When I recognize that the Lord has just used me to bless someone, encourage them, or to meet their needs, I often thank Him. It is a treat to be used by the Lord, and brings great joy to my heart.

Love is large and incredibly patient. Love is gentle and consistently kind to all. It refuses to be jealous when blessing comes to someone else. Love does not brag about one's achievements nor inflate its own importance.

Love does not traffic in shame and disrespect, nor selfishly seek its own honor. Love is not easily irritated or quick to take offense.

Love joyfully celebrates honesty and finds no delight in what is wrong. Love is a safe place of shelter, for it never stops believing the best for others. Love never takes failure as defeat, for it never gives up. (1 Corinthians 13:4-7)

Peter and Cornelius

As the early church began to pick up speed and the disciples began preaching the gospel to the neighboring cities and countries, Peter was sent to the Gentiles. One afternoon after receiving an intense vision from the Lord, Peter was directed by the Holy Spirit to go with three men he had never met before. By faith, Peter obeyed and came to the house of Cornelius, a Roman military captain (a Gentile).

> *As Peter was in deep thought, trying to interpret the vision, the Spirit said to him, "Go downstairs now, for three men are looking for you. Don't hesitate to go with them, because I have sent them."* (Acts 10:19-20)

> *The Spirit told me to accompany them with no questions asked. These six brothers here with me made the trip, and we entered into the home of the man who had sent for me.* (Acts 11:12)

The story unfolds beautifully with Cornelius and his entire family becoming baptized in the Holy Spirit, speaking in tongues, coming to salvation, and being baptized in water (Acts 10). Because of Peter's quick obedience to the Holy Spirit and love for others, Cornelius and his entire household were saved.

> *This [is what] I command you: that you love and unselfishly seek the best for one another.* (John 15:17 AMP)

Mail Lady and a Big Hug

Being in my forties now, I will be the first to admit that I am not the most tech-savvy person. Finding my way around a smart phone is simple enough, but participating in social media is a whole different story for me. Many years ago, I had a Facebook account, but for various reasons, I deleted it. About two years ago, the Lord asked me to reopen an account, so I did. A few months after that, He nudged me to really get going with it. Clumsily I began to press buttons here and there, trying my best to understand the app. Finally, things began to make sense as I uploaded some family photos and started to slowly connect with those around me.

About a week later, I noticed a thread from the neighborhood group I had joined talking about how our mail carrier's mother had just passed away. My heart was moved with compassion, and I prayed for her. The mail lady and I had met before as I ran a letter out to her or she brought a box to me, but I did not have her phone number or any way to reach her directly. A few days later, as I was heading out to run errands, I saw her loading the mailboxes up front by the entrance to our community. Immediately in my heart, the Spirit of the Lord said,

Hug her.

Absolutely, I responded in my heart.

Pulling the van over, I parked. Not sure exactly what to say, but knowing I was being sent to love on her, I trusted the Holy Spirit would break the water as soon as I opened my mouth. He did of course, and as I gave my condolences to her regarding her mother, she immediately began to tear up. She explained how she was feeling and what a tough year this had already been for her. Stepping toward her, I asked,

"Can I give you a hug?"

She agreed, and we embraced. Before I left, I assured her she could stop by to talk or have coffee anytime. She knew where we lived. It seemed she just needed to be heard for a few minutes and receive some tangible love from the Father.

As I drove away, I was so thankful I had listened to the Holy Spirit about getting onto Facebook so I could see the message about her mother. By God's grace, my quick obedience allowed Holy Spirit to use me as a messenger of God's love. Praise Adonai!

> *No one has ever gazed upon the fullness of God's splendor.* **But if we love one another**, *God makes his permanent home in us, and we make our permanent home in him, and his love is brought to its full expression in us.* (1 John 4:12)

Ten Dollars at the Department Store

These days, I hardly ever shop at department stores. Amazon has truly taken the world by storm. However, one afternoon last year my husband and I were out shopping together. At the register, the cashier mentioned applying a coupon for us, commenting how she had a hard time not saving folks money whenever she could. This spoke volumes to me about her character. She was going out of her way to help us and to help others.

As my heart quietly reflected on her kindness, the Spirit of the Lord dropped this very clear impression into my spirit,

Give her a ten-dollar bill.

Yes Lord, I thought.

Quickly going over the bills in my wallet mentally, I knew I did not have a ten, but I wanted to obey. As she continued to ring us up, I casually leaned over to Sam and whispered,

"Do you have a ten? The Holy Spirit just asked me to give it to her."

"Yes, here you go." Sam said as he handed me a ten from his wallet.

As she finished up, I gave it to her and said something like,

"As you were ringing us up just now, the Lord asked me to give you ten dollars. Thank you for how kind you have been to so many people. God sees you and He loves you."

Her eyes got so big and the smile on her face was priceless. She could hardly believe it, and responded with something like,

"Oh my goodness thank you! I can't believe this! Now I will be able to get lunch."

> **As the Lord nudges us, remember all we must do is obey. And what a blessing to be used by the Lord!**

Bless her heart. I had no idea she didn't have lunch money, but God knew. And although not everyone noticed her kindness, Abba wanted to thank her. It was a simple ten dollars, but I know she felt God's love that day. As we walked out of the department store, Sam mentioned that particular ten-dollar bill had been sitting on his nightstand for weeks. He said he just felt led to grab it before we left the house that day. Isn't God amazing?

As the Lord nudges us, remember all we must do is obey. And what a blessing to be used by the Lord!

Your ears will hear a word behind you, "This is the way, walk in it," whenever you turn to the right or to the left. (Isaiah 30:21 AMP)

Chapter 10

Led by Dreams from the Lord

T he Holy Spirit can also lead us by way of dreams. Sometimes they are called prophetic dreams. You can see the Lord using dreams to guide people throughout the entire Bible (Genesis 37:5-11, Genesis 40:8, Daniel 2, Matthew 1:20, Acts 16:9-10). These dreams seem to be flashes of the future. Sometimes the dreams show something good to come, while other dreams show something bad to come.

Over the years, the Holy Spirit has given me and my family many dreams like this. At first, we didn't realize what they were, so we did nothing about the dreams. If something bad happened in the dream, it seemed to later happen in real life. Yikes! And if something good happened in the dream, it would not seem to happen in real life. Why?

Then several years ago, the Lord sent a woman of God into our lives to explain dreams from the Lord and how we as believers in the Messiah can do something about them. We immediately began applying the verses she showed us in Scripture, and it worked! Not all dreams are from the Lord, but when they are, there is a quickening in your spirit that you just cannot shake. Abba will remind you in the morning or it will be *so* real that you will wake up in the middle of the night. When this happens, please pay attention. This is most likely a dream from the Lord, and He wants you to do something with it.

*But when the truth-giving Spirit comes, he will unveil the reality of every truth within you. He won't speak on his own, but only what he hears from the Father, and **he will reveal prophetically to you what is to come.*** (John 16:13)

Blessing Dreams

There seems to be two kinds of prophetic dreams from the Lord – blessing and warning dreams. The first kind I call blessing dreams. These are dreams with a flash of something good that God wants for you or for someone else. An example of a blessing dream takes place in Joesph's life when the Lord encouraged Joseph in a dream to take Mary as his wife (Matthew 1:20-24). I have found that if we agree with what was seen in a dream, it is the same as giving God our yes. What I mean by agree, is to pray and keep praying for whatever blessing or good thing the Lord showed you in the dream until it manifests in this realm (pray for days, months, or years until it happens). When one of my kids, my husband, or I wake up and remember a blessing dream from the Lord, we usually tell each other. Then we agree with the Lord in prayer for the blessing.

> *"Yes, Lord! We agree to this happening in our lives (or in this person's life). We allow it. Let Your will be done on earth as it is in heaven."* (Matthew 6:10)

As we have continued to believe and pray with faith, my family and I have seen many things come to pass in the earth exactly or very close to what the Lord has shown us in these blessing dreams. Some of you may think that praying for God's will to be done on earth might be a waste of time, as many people and even some pastors say that God is in control of this world (meaning if He wants it to happen, it will happen). Although God is sovereign, He gives each one of us free will. And sadly, many people choose to sin with their free will every day. Yeshua Himself said that satan is the ruler of this dark world (John 14:30). Many bad things happen in the world every day – things that God allowed, but did not want to happen. I believe that is why Yeshua asked us to pray for God's will to be done in the earth, because His will does not automatically happen in the earth.

> *Pray, then, in this way: "Our Father, who is in heaven, Hallowed be Your name. Your kingdom come,* **Your will be done on earth as it is in heaven.**" (Matthew 6:9-10 AMP)

So if you receive a blessing dream from the Lord, please take it seriously. Talk with the Lord about it, and ask Him to bring it to pass in the earth. I keep a dream journal, which helps me remember to pray for what the Lord has shown me in dreams over the years. Some blessing dreams take time to manifest, so please be diligent in prayer whether for weeks, months, or even years.

> *So I say to you,* ***ask and keep on asking,*** *and it will be given to you; seek and keep on seeking, and you will find; knock and keep on knocking, and the door will be opened to you.*
>
> *For everyone who keeps on asking [persistently], receives; and he who keeps on seeking [persistently], finds; and to*

him who keeps on knocking [persistently], the door will be opened. (Luke 11:9-11 AMP)

Warning Dreams

The other type of prophetic dreams given by the Lord I call warning dreams. You can see examples of warning dreams in Scripture as well. Joseph, Yeshua's earthly father, was warned two separate times in dreams from the Lord to protect Yeshua as a child and to go certain places with Him (Matthew 2:12-13 and Matthew 2:22). In the same way, God has periodically given us warning dreams that flash something bad the devil has planned against us or against someone we know. It is usually something the Lord does *not* want to happen in the earth. We see these warning dreams as God's grace to us. When we have a warning dream, we usually talk about it in the morning, repent of any sin that may be in our hearts, and agree in prayer against whatever we saw in the dream.

It is important to begin with repenting of any known (or unknown) sin as unrepentant sin can leave an open door for the enemy to attack you or your family. That is why we repent first.

> **So submit to [the authority of] God.** *Resist the devil [stand firm against him] and he will flee from you.* (James 4:7 AMP)

Once our hearts are clean, we pray to the Father taking the authority He gave us over the demonic.

"Father, we do not allow this thing to happen. We do not agree with it. We pray against this in Yeshua's name. Let Your will be done on earth as it is in heaven." (Matthew 6:10)

Then we give satan a strong rebuke,

"We take authority over you, satan and over all the power of darkness, and we forbid you to cause sickness to us or this person (or death – whatever bad thing that was seen in the dream). We do not allow you to do this in Yeshua's name."

Next, we often ask the Father to send His angels to assist in the situation and provide complete protection. At times, we also end by praying in tongues. Holy Spirit knows exactly how to pray against the devil's schemes.

Here are some Bible verses to support what we are doing and why.

Receive this truth: Whatever you forbid on earth will be considered to be forbidden in heaven, and whatever you release on earth will be considered to be released in heaven. (Matthew 18:18)

And in a similar way, the Holy Spirit takes hold of us in our human frailty to empower us in our weakness. For example, at times we don't even know how to pray, or know the best things to ask for. But the Holy Spirit rises up within us to super-intercede on our behalf, pleading to God with emotional sighs too deep for words. (Romans 8:26)

By God's grace, handling warning dreams this way has helped tremendously. After praying and rebuking this way, most of the time the bad things we saw in warning dreams have not happened. Praise Adonai!

Now you understand that I have imparted to you my authority to trample over his kingdom. You will trample upon every demon before you and overcome every power Satan possesses. Absolutely nothing will harm you as you walk in this authority. (Luke 10:19)

When We Did Nothing

Some of you may be thinking this is a little over board. However, before my family and I knew how to pray against bad things that we saw in dreams, we very distinctly remember a terrible thing happening to us in real life that we had seen in a warning dream a few months prior, but we did nothing. Now we know what to do. The Lord has given us keys to His Kingdom and I believe He wants each one of His followers to use them.

I will give you the keys (authority) of the kingdom of heaven; and whatever you bind [forbid, declare to be improper and unlawful] on earth will have [already] been bound in heaven, and whatever you loose [permit, declare lawful] on earth will have [already] been loosed in heaven. (Matthew 16:19 AMP)

> ## The Lord has given us keys to His Kingdom and I believe He wants each one of His followers to use them.

And to be transparent with you, one time, even after praying against what seemed to be a warning dream, the bad thing still happened to us. Recently, one of my friends mentioned a similar situation happening to her as well – where she prayed against a bad dream, but it still happened. Perhaps at times the Lord uses these warning dreams to simply prepare us for what is coming next? I do not have all the answers, but I *do* know that when we began praying against what was happening in these warning dreams, many bad things stopped happening in our lives and those around us.

Additionally, if the prophetic dream is about someone else, I like to ask permission from Holy Spirit before calling the person. If He gives me the okay, then I call the person in my dream and explain it. Most of the time, the person is very happy for the call and agrees with me for or against whatever was seen in the dream. However, at times, I have received warning dreams about someone where the Lord did *not* want me to reach out to the person in the dream. Perhaps the insight was just for me to know and intercede on their behalf, or perhaps the person would not have received it well. In these instances, I just pray on my own.

The FAA and Three Stamps

Almost three years ago now, my husband left the FAA after their mandate to take the covid shot. As I mentioned earlier, we did not have peace about the shot. This is when Sam left the FAA, and we moved to North Carolina. He found a temporary job at the time, but about six months later, the FAA dropped the mandate. We began to pray about Sam re-applying, as his skills as an air traffic controller were still fresh, and it paid much better than the current job he was at. During this time frame, the Lord gave me a very clear blessing dream of Sam getting an offer letter from the FAA with a date on it. The date was about three months into the future, and the letter had three stamps in the upper right-hand corner. Waking up, I instantly knew this was God's answer for Sam to re-apply. I told Sam right away, and he chuckled and said something like,

> *"You wouldn't know this Honey, but there are three departments my application will have to be approved by. I believe that is what the three stamps represent."*

Wow! I had no idea of these three departments, but the three stamps *were* one of the highlights in the dream. By faith, Sam re-applied to the FAA, and by faith, we diligently prayed for three months that they would re-hire him. Sure enough, three months later, the FAA reached out to Sam, offering him a job. Amazingly, the day they reached out to Sam was within one day of the date I saw in the dream. *One day!* The Lord was totally directing us with that blessing dream, and even guiding us with a close estimate of when we would receive the answer. How gracious is our God!

*He was so kind, so gracious to me. Because of his passion
toward me, he made everything right and he restored me.*
(Psalm 116:5)

Long Driveway and a Phone Call

One night, I had a warning dream about one of my friends. In the
dream, I saw what looked like a demonic being walking down the street
near her home. Then he began walking down her long driveway toward
her house. Awakening with a start, I instantly knew in my spirit that
the Lord was warning me about a demonic plan against this woman
and her family. The symbolism of it being in her driveway but not
inside her home yet meant there was time but not much. I called her
up, and she agreed to pray against this demonic attack with me. We
bound (forbid) satan from attacking her and her family, and we loosed
(allowed) angelic assistance from the Lord to protect her and her family.
In addition, we thanked the Lord for the warning and asked Him to sur-
round this woman and her family with His protection. Peace followed.
The attack never happened. Praise Adonai.

How to Interpret Your Dreams

Learning to interpret your dreams from the Father can take time, but I
have found the closer you walk with the Lord, the easier it is to interpret your dreams. And remember, not every dream you have is from
the Lord. When it is, you will just know. There is a quickening or
urgency about dreams from the Lord. When you receive a dream from
the Lord, it is wise not to run straight to your pastor or good friend for

the interpretation. First, ask Abba what the dream means and how to pray about it. He will guide you. I have found that the person receiving the dream from the Lord is usually the best person to interpret it. Here are some consistencies in dreams from the Lord that have helped me and my family over the years. Lord willing, they will help you as well.

> **I have found that the person receiving the dream from the Lord is usually the best person to interpret it.**

- Try to remember what was said by you or by someone else in the dream. Write these things down quickly, word for word. Usually what is said is key.

- Was anything highlighted to you in the dream (like the three stamps in the FAA dream to me)? A picture, a person, a street name? Ask Abba about these things specifically.

- Did someone say a date or a location or a name?

- Where were you in the dream? Was it in the present or did the kids look older (years from now)? This has meant happening soon, or happening later in life for us.

- Did you sense something obvious that wasn't said by anyone, but you just knew or understood? This usually bears weight with the interpretation.

- Reference Bible verses if something seems similar to what you saw or heard in the dream. Read the verse in context (whole chapter or book around it), not just the actual verse. This has helped with interpretation before.

- If there is a person in the dream that is highlighted, but it doesn't make sense to you, look up the meaning of their name. God could be highlighting the meaning of the name, not the actual person.

- White usually represents God or Him making us white, in preparation for His Kingdom (white sandals, towels, dresses).

- Snakes, spiders, alligators, demons, darkness, usually represents satan or what he is planning to do. These are usually warning dreams.

- If something is floating in air or levitating that usually means witchcraft.

- Anything with Disney usually represents witchcraft.

- The color orange has represented the sin of anger in my dream (orange snake, orange spiders).

- Repeat dreams often have to do with your past or your childhood regarding an open door of sin that you have but may not be aware of. Ask for extra wisdom, and repent as the Lord guides you, so the door is shut tight.

- An old building has represented the Old Testament and a new building has represented the New Testament in one of my dreams.

- Being barefoot has represented something in real life catching me off guard.

- Someone with white hair/aged in a dream has represented someone with wise council, someone who could be trusted. God wanted me to trust this person in real life, however what's funny is this person wasn't very old in real life. Amazing how God sees things.

- Zip codes and dates usually mean just that, a physical location or an actual date.

- If something (snake, demon, scorpion) is in the back yard/front yard or driveway of someone's house (or of your own house) it usually means the attack is coming but not there yet. If it is already inside the house, it is usually a bigger and deeper-rooted sin, but still possible to remove with prayer and repentance. Ask for wisdom and obey right away.

- If you see a friend or a loved one die in a dream, ask the Lord for wisdom. Many times, this has meant actual death, and many times we've prayed against it and the person has lived. Praise Adonai! However, at times it has also meant metaphoric death, where Abba was asking me to give up a friendship and it *felt* like a death to me. So definitely ask Abba for wisdom.

There are more examples I could share, but hopefully this will help you get started as you begin (or continue) to analyze and interpret your dreams from the Lord. He is so gracious to give us these dreams, and is more than happy to help us with the interpretation. May we all partner with Him as we see the day approaching!

> *This is what I will do in the last days — I will pour out my Spirit on everybody and cause your sons and daughters to prophesy, and your young men will see visions, and your old men will experience dreams from God.*
>
> *The Holy Spirit will come upon all my servants, men and women alike, and they will prophesy.* (Acts 2:17-18)

Chapter 11

Led to Preach the Gospel

O ne of the last things Yeshua said to His followers before leaving the earth was to preach the gospel to all nations. Spending time with the Father in prayer and in reading His Word can help us share the gospel, but Yeshua also said He would send the Holy Spirit to help us and empower us to share the gospel with others.

> *Now you must go into all the nations and preach repen-*
> *tance and forgiveness of sins so that they will turn to me.*
> *Start right here in Jerusalem, for you are my witnesses*
> *and have seen for yourselves all that has transpired.*
>
> *I will send the fulfillment of the Father's promise to you, so*
> *stay here in the city until you are clothed with the mighty*
> *power of heaven.* (Luke 24:47-49)

The Lord doesn't just want us to be saved, He wants us to be fully equipped with the baptism of the Holy Spirit, knowing it will help us preach the gospel with love and boldness.

Although we covered the baptism of the Holy Spirit in an earlier chapter, I wanted to bring it up again here because it made such a difference for me in sharing the gospel with others. The Lord doesn't just want us to be saved, He wants us to be fully equipped with the baptism of the Holy Spirit, knowing it will help us preach the gospel with love and boldness. Before I was baptized in the Holy Spirit, sharing the gospel seemed difficult. Starting conversations and knowing who to share with was challenging for me. However, after being baptized in the Holy Spirit, sharing the gospel became much easier for me. There is boldness, love, and wisdom that flows now. I believe this difference is the Holy Spirit empowering and helping me as I follow His lead.

> *For John baptized with water, but you will be baptized and empowered and united with the Holy Spirit, not long from now.* (Acts 1:5 AMP)

The Disciples' Boldness

In the Book of Acts, we see a transformation in the Messiah's followers *after* the baptism of the Holy Spirit. After Yeshua rose from the dead, but prior to the Day of Pentecost, the disciples were still concerned about the religious leaders and were meeting behind locked doors (John 20:19). However, on the Day of Pentecost, *after* the Holy Spirit came upon the disciples, they were all filled with and equipped by the Holy Spirit and began speaking in other tongues as the Holy Spirit inspired them. With boldness from Holy Spirit, Peter preached a very powerful sermon to those who were in Jerusalem. The Scripture says that about 3,000 souls were added to the body of believers that day (Acts 2). Glory to God!

Two chapters later in the Book of Acts, another example emerges of the Holy Spirit bringing boldness to Peter and John. They were no longer hiding behind locked doors. They had been out preaching the gospel and because of it, they were brought before the Sanhedrin (Jewish high court) for questioning.

> **The council members were astonished as they witnessed the bold courage of Peter and John,** *especially when they discovered that they were just ordinary men who had never had religious training. Then they began to understand the effect Jesus had on them simply by spending time with him.* (Acts 14:13)

A short time later, some disciples were gathered together and were praying about the oppression they were experiencing in the city, and the power of the Holy Spirit filled them again with fresh boldness and courage.

> *And when they had prayed, the place where they were meeting together was shaken; and they were all filled with the Holy Spirit and began to speak the word of God* **with boldness and courage.** (Acts 4:31 AMP)

Time to Be Bold

As we continue spending time with Abba in prayer and reading His Word, we foster a closeness with Him like never before. The baptism of the Holy Spirit helps immensely, and then day by day, the Holy Spirit will begin to use us more and more. He will guide us to step out and be bold with the gospel message. At times He may ask us to share a testimony from our life about what the Father has done for us. Other times, He may ask us to share a meal with someone or give them something to drink. At times He may need us to quote His Word to someone regarding sin or other hard topics. Whatever the person needs, the Holy Spirit knows and He will guide us. If it seems impossible or awkward to you, or your heart begins to race, just ask Abba for the next step or a way to start the conversation with the person. He loves you and the other person incredibly! Just do your best to share the gospel *as Holy Spirit leads you*. As you step out in faith, the boldness and compassion will flow.

It is so important not to become discouraged because of rejection.

When I am being led to share the gospel with someone, it is usually received well, but not always. As we follow the Holy Spirit and share the gospel with others, it is so important not to become discouraged because of rejection. At times, when Yeshua shared the gospel, He was rejected, and so were His followers. Rejection did not mean Yeshua did something wrong, and *if we are being led by the Holy Spirit* and are rejected, it does not mean we did anything wrong either.

*He was despised and rejected by men, a man of deep
sorrows who was no stranger to suffering and grief. We
hid our faces from him in disgust and considered him a
nobody, not worthy of respect.* (Isaiah 53:3)

Street Lady and a Chili Dog

Last year, the Holy Spirit nudged our family to start ministering to the
community more. He guided us to the streets of Jacksonville to share
God's love and some food with the people who don't have homes.
Sam, the kids, and I grill up the chili dogs in our kitchen and add Bible
verses to the outside wrapping. Before we head out, we load the van
with waters, new socks, chips, fruit, and a wagon. Then we pray over
everything, asking the Lord for protection and guidance in ministering
to His people that day.

One afternoon as the family and I were passing out chili dogs, a
woman caught my eye. I felt led to give her a chili dog. She smiled and
asked if I had been out on the streets two years ago saying the same
message (I was telling her how much God loved her). In those moments,
I felt Holy Spirit's words coming out of my spirit. I responded confidently with something like,

*"No, I wasn't here two years ago, but this shows me the Lord is after
you. He loves you dearly, and is sending me two years after the first
person to tell you again how much God loves you."*

We hugged, and my family and I continued on our way, passing out
more chili dogs, socks, and bottles of water. I'm not sure what choice
she will make, but Lord willing our conversation watered a seed that
was already planted.

Everyone who reaps these souls for eternal life will receive a reward. Both those who plant spiritual seeds and those who reap the spiritual harvest will celebrate together with great joy! And this confirms the saying, 'One sows the seed and another reaps the harvest.' (John 4:36-37)

Street Lady and a Chili Dog

> We don't need to "go-witness" because we are a
> witness wherever we go, every day of our lives.

Although ministering on the streets is something we feel led to do, God can and does use us every day to preach the gospel with love and boldness no matter where we are. We don't need to "go-witness" because we *are* a witness wherever we go, every day of our lives. My dad and mom say this to the Lord in the morning, and I often do as well.

"Good morning, Lord, how can I help You today?"

Then as we go about our day, we are ready for those go-time moments when the Spirit guides us to reach out to others. May we all be ready to share God's love, His grace, His forgiveness, and His gospel of salvation with others.

> *Jesus ordered us to preach and warn the people that God had appointed him to be the judge of the living and the dead. And not only us, but all of the prophets agree in their writings that everyone who believes in him receives complete forgiveness of sins through the power of his name.* (Acts 10:42-43)

Chapter 12

Led to Heal the Sick

We touched on how the Holy Spirit gives us supernatural love and boldness to preach the gospel. Now let's talk about how He can lead us to heal the sick as well.

> *And these miracle signs will accompany **those who believe**: They will drive out demons in the power of my name. They will speak in tongues. They will be supernaturally protected from snakes and from drinking anything poisonous. **And they will lay hands on the sick and heal them.*** (Mark 16:17-18)

Cessationism in the Church Today

It doesn't take long to find miracles and healings throughout the entire Bible. In the Old Testament, we see Elijah and Elisha working miracles through the Lord's power (1 Kings 17 & 2 Kings 2). In the New Testament, we see Yeshua working mighty miracles, including many healings. Later in the New Testament, we see Peter, Stephen, and Paul working similar miracles and healings in Yeshua's name.

Although many believers agree that the Messiah's followers performed these miracles and healings in the first century, for some reason they also believe the power of the Holy Spirit, including healing, is no longer in affect today. This belief, dare I say false doctrine, is called Cessationism. It teaches that the Father no longer works through individuals regarding tongues, prophecy, and healings today. This ideology claims this all stopped after the apostles died. Unfortunately, many Christians believe this and even some pastors preach it. However, the Scriptures do not support Cessationism or even allude to it.

As we have discussed in a previous chapter, I speak in tongues and so do many other believers in the Messiah today. In fact, Paul spoke in tongues, and he said he wished all of us spoke in tongues (1 Corinthians 14:5). It helps my walk with the Lord immensely (1 Corinthians 14:4). In addition, like we discussed in the dream chapter, the Father can speak prophetically through dreams today. He has done this with our family many times. He also gives words of prophecy, or tongues with interpretation, which is like prophecy to various believers today.

> Just because someone has not experienced tongues, prophecy, healings, or other gifts of the Spirit does not mean they have ceased.

I have received correct prophetic words from many believers in the Messiah in the past few years. All this to say that the gifts of the Holy Spirit are very much alive and well today. Just because someone has not experienced tongues, prophecy, healings, or other gifts of the Spirit does not mean they have ceased. Someday they will cease, but not yet.

Love never fails. But as for prophecies, they will pass away; as for tongues, they will cease; as for the gift of special knowledge, it will pass away. For we know in part, and we prophesy in part.

But when that which is complete and perfect comes, that which is incomplete and partial will pass away. (1 Corinthians 13:8-10 AMP)

Let's look up the original Hebrew word. In the Strongs Concordance, "perfect" here is H8549 *tamim*, and means complete, whole, entire, blameless. So, I believe Paul is saying that when that which is perfect comes back, the Messiah, we will no longer need these imperfect gifts of the Holy Spirit. Until then, however, they will remain. In the meantime, what a blessing these gifts of the Spirit are. If you have not experienced the gifts of the Holy Spirit yet, you can ask the Father to baptize you with the Holy Spirit right now. If you have already done this, you can always ask for more of the Holy Spirit.

If imperfect parents know how to lovingly take care of their children and give them what they need, **how much more will the perfect heavenly Father give the Holy Spirit's fullness when his children ask him.** (Luke 11:13)

The Holy Spirit will decide what gifts to give us. Then we must be faithful to use them as we are led.

All these things [the gifts, the achievements, the abilities, the empowering] are brought about by one and the same

Spirit, distributing to each one individually just as He chooses. (1 Corinthians 12:11 AMP)

There are many accounts all over the world in which followers of the Messiah have preached the gospel and signs and wonders have followed them including healings, resurrection from the dead, demonic deliverance, and more. In fact, my own family has prayed for and received three miraculous healings from the Lord in just the last six years. A friend of mine also experienced a miraculous healing and so did her daughter. The gifts of the Holy Spirit are very much alive and well today.

> *I tell you this timeless truth:* **The person who follows me in faith,** *believing in me, will do the same mighty miracles that I do—even greater miracles than these because I go to be with my Father!* (John 14:12)

Ananias and Saul's Healing

Shortly after Yeshua's ascension into Heaven, the apostles and the early believers in Yeshua continued to spread the good news of the gospel. At the time, there was a man named Saul who was a devout pharisee. He was going around persecuting the new believers in Yeshua. He honestly thought he was doing God a favor, but was confused by who Yeshua really was. On one of Saul's trips to continue persecuting the Messiah, he received a life-altering visitation from Yeshua, Himself. Saul was on his way to a city called Damascus when it happened. Because of the brilliance of the light surrounding Yeshua during this visitation, Saul became blind and remained so for several days (Acts 8-9).

The Lord was more than ready to use Saul for His glory on earth. However, He first needed a brave soul to go to Saul and love on him, to heal him physically, and to baptize him in the Holy Spirit. Ananias, a follower of Yeshua, was this brave soul. The Lord came to Ananias in a vision and explained to him the assignment to go to Saul. Praise the Lord for Ananias' courage and obedience.

> *Now in Damascus there was a disciple named Ananias; and the Lord said to him in a vision, "Ananias."*
>
> *And he answered, "Here I am, Lord."*
>
> *And the Lord said to him, "Get up and go to the street called Straight, and ask at the house of Judas for a man from Tarsus named Saul; for he is praying, and in a vision he has seen a man named Ananias come in and place his hands on him, so that he may regain his sight."* (Acts 9:10-12 AMP)

Ananias obediently came to Paul and even called him brother. He demonstrated the Father's love and laid his hands on Paul for healing. Scripture states something like scales fell off Paul's eyes and his sight was restored. He received the power of the Holy Spirit and was later water baptized as well (Acts 9).

We are not meant to rely on our own strength or understanding to heal someone.

One of the things the Father has taught me, is that healing miracles do not seem to follow a pattern. We are not meant to rely on our own strength or understanding to heal someone. We are to follow the leading of the Holy Spirit every time. Think about it. Sometimes Yeshua would use mud, sometimes spit, and sometimes He would just say the word and the person would be healed. Here, Ananias laid his hands on Saul and the scales fell off. So as we follow the leading of the Holy Spirit to heal others, it's important that we do not lean on our own understanding. Instead, every time may we lean into whatever impression or nudge we feel from the Lord regarding the person or the situation.

Trust in and rely confidently on the Lord with all your heart and do not rely on your own insight or understanding. *In all your ways know and acknowledge and recognize Him, and He will make your paths straight and smooth.* (Proverbs 3:5-6 AMP)

Then Jesus spat on the ground and made some clay with his saliva. Then he anointed the blind man's eyes with the clay.

And he said to the blind man, "Now go and wash the clay from your eyes in the ritual pool of Siloam." So he went and washed his face and as he came back, he could see for the first time in his life! (John 9:6-7)

Prayer for Healing and "Pop Rockets"

About six years ago, my thyroid was really hurting. The herbal remedies were not working, and the synthetic medication I was on for years
seemed to be complicating things and bringing on terrible side effects
as well. Back then, I wasn't very confident about the Lord healing me.
I believed He *could* heal me... I just wasn't sure if He would. Because
of this, although I prayed for healing, I spent a lot of time on herbal
and natural remedies. Year after year, tea after tincture, prayer after
prayer, my thyroid kept getting worse. I was exhausted and my faith
was small by then.

About that time, several ladies and I felt led to pray together. Prayer
requests were taken, and we began. My request was that the Lord
would heal my thyroid. We prayed for one another in turn, and when
it was my turn to be prayed for, my thyroid instantly began to pop
and crackle in my throat. It felt similar to swallowing those fun can-
dies called Pop Rockets, but softer. Hardly able to contain myself, I
stammered,

*"Keep-keep praying, Ladies! My throat is warm and it's crackling
and popping!"*

The ladies kept praying and praising the Lord as my thyroid gland
was being healed. For the next ten minutes or so my thyroid remained
warm and kept gently popping. I believe Heavenly Father was opening
the nodules that had collected on my thyroid gland over the years,
allowing the blood to flow again. By faith, and by His direction, I went
off my thyroid medication the very next day. To this day I am healed
and off all medication. In addition, my labs came back normal. Praise
Adonai! That day I felt the Father's love like never before. It was personal and so life changing! I don't remember having a lot of faith that

day, but I did have a little. I believe the others had faith as well. We simply felt led to pray that day, and the Lord worked through us to manifest His miracle, healing power. I am forever grateful to the Lord for His love and grace.

> He told them, "It was because of your lack of faith. I promise you, **if you have faith inside of you no bigger than the size of a small mustard seed**, you can say to this mountain, 'Move away from here and go over there,' and you will see it move! There is nothing you couldn't do! (Matthew 17:20)

Music Teacher and a Migraine

Shortly after my thyroid was healed, my daughter and I were at her weekly piano lesson. At some point after we arrived, the teacher mentioned having a migraine. In those moments, I felt the Holy Spirit nudge me to lay hands on her for healing and to place my hands right where it hurt. I asked her something like,

"Would you mind if I prayed for healing? May I lay my hands on your head where it hurts?"

She seemed a little surprised, but agreed. Asking her where it hurt most, I laid my hands on that part of her head and prayed a simple prayer for healing. Shortly afterward she said something like,

"I felt something in your hands as you prayed. My head got warm and the pain has begun to leave."

> **Abba seems to enjoy mixing up the nudges in order for us to depend on Him for direction.**

Praise God for working through me that day! I was thrilled to be used by the Lord and so grateful to experience again how deeply God loves each one of us. It is important to remember that Abba seems to enjoy mixing up the nudges in order for us to depend on Him (lay hands, say this, do that). So when you feel led to heal someone, please pay attention to the Lord's direction. The Holy Spirit will guide you. Just follow His lead.

Times When Nothing Happens

I wanted to add this section for transparency. There have been times when I have prayed for healing with compassion for people and faith for God to heal them, but nothing visible seemed to happen. Over the years I have wondered,

Why didn't it work, Lord?

Understanding now that we are to be led by the Holy Spirit in all things, I cannot honestly say that I was being led to heal every single time I tried. Most likely, I was attempting to heal on my own in those cases. And remember, Yeshua only did the will of the Father – so if I was not doing the will of our Father, that is most likely why it did not work. I'm still learning and growing. But what I do know is that often when I feel the clear signal from the Lord to lay hands for healing, or pray for healing, God *does* heal. Praise Adonai.

Are there any sick among you? Then ask the elders of the church to come and pray over the sick and anoint them with oil in the name of our Lord. And the prayer of faith will heal the sick and the Lord will raise them up, and if they have committed sins they will be forgiven. (James 5:14-15)

Ask and Keep on Asking

My family and I have also received healings from the Lord by not giving up in prayer when we felt like healing was His will. When we prayed fervently for days, months, and even years, my family has received miraculous healings by the hand of the Lord. One healing was for our daughter, and one was for our son. We also received an additional healing by way of a doctor finally discovering the cause of something we had been praying about for years. The Lord used modern medicine to heal this one, but still a huge answer to prayer. Whether you feel led to pray in the moment and instant healing comes, or whether you feel led to ask and keep on asking, just follow the leading of the Holy Spirit.

*So I say to you, **ask and keep on asking**, and it will be given to you; **seek and keep on seeking**, and you will find; **knock and keep on knocking**, and the door will be opened to you.*

For everyone who keeps on asking [persistently], receives; and he who keeps on seeking [persistently], finds; and to him who keeps on knocking [persistently], the door will be opened. (Luke 11:9-10 AMP)

Chapter 13

Led to Cast Out Demons

O ver the years, some of you may have heard about or read stories from the Bible of Yeshua casting out demons from many people. As a child I read these stories in the Bible and remember thinking,

Wow, there certainly were a lot of demons on the earth back then. Wonder where they all went?

I thought this because all the believers I knew at the time (including myself) were not casting out any demons or even talking about them. Years later, after I was baptized in the Holy Spirit and studied the Scriptures more thoroughly, I realized the demons did not go anywhere. They are still on the earth today oppressing and tormenting people. They enjoy hiding behind names of diseases, people's bad habits, drugs, violence, and many other things. But these demonic spirits are still present today, roaming the earth, trying to hurt and kill people. In Scripture, we see Yeshua casting these demonic spirits out of people, and telling His followers to do the same.

> Demonic spirits enjoy hiding behind names of diseases, people's bad habits, drugs, violence, and many other things.

And as you go, preach this message: 'Heaven's kingdom realm is accessible, close enough to touch.' You must continually bring healing to lepers and to those who are sick, and **make it your habit to break off the demonic presence from people**, *and raise the dead back to life. Freely you have received the power of the kingdom, so freely release it to others.* (Matthew 10:7-8)

This kind of authority may seem overwhelming at first, but remember from Luke 24:49 that the baptism of the Holy Spirit brings power. One of the definitions of this power in Strongs 1411 is *"the power consisting in or resting upon armies, forces, and hosts."*

Just like the Holy Spirit may lead us to heal someone, He may also lead us to cast out a demonic spirit from someone. He will show us who needs deliverance and will guide us. Just to be transparent, at times we may need deliverance ourselves from demonic oppression. Later in this chapter, I will give examples of how we have successfully rebuked demonic spirits when we were led to by the Holy Spirit.

Yeshua and the Demoniac

In the Books of Matthew, Mark, and Luke, we see a story unfold in which Yeshua was led to take a trip across the Sea of Galilee to deliver a man being harassed by many demons. Upon their arrival, the man was naked and had been cutting himself and living among the tombs. He rushed to Yeshua and the demons possessing him began to speak through his mouth, addressing Yeshua as the Son of God. They recognized His authority to cast them out. They made it quite clear they did not want to go to the abyss or out of the region. Yeshua agreed, and they left the man and entered a herd of pigs nearby. After being delivered, the man put clothes on and was in his right mind again, sitting at Yeshua's feet (Matthew 8, Mark 5, and Luke 8). The man was set free! Hallelujah!

> *When he saw Jesus from a distance, he ran to him and threw himself down before him, shouting at the top of his lungs, "Leave me alone, Jesus, Son of the Most High God! Swear in God's name that you won't torture me!"*
>
> *(For Jesus had already said to him, "Come out of that man, you demon spirit!")* (Mark 5:6-8)
>
> *When they found Jesus, they saw the demonized man sitting there, properly clothed and in his right mind.* (Mark 5:15a)

If we are careful to read this story in context, there are many nuggets to glean regarding how to rebuke demons. First, we read that prior to Yeshua's arrival on the shore to help this man, He told His disciples,

> *"Let's cross over to the other side of the lake."* (Mark 4:35b)

Since the Father sent Yeshua to help deliver someone from demons, we know that He can send us, too.

This tells us that Yeshua was being sent by the Father. How do we know this? Earlier, Yeshua mentioned that He does and says nothing on His own, but only that which the Father tells Him (John 5:19 and John 12:49). That means at some point, Father God led Yeshua to make this trip across the lake. Since the Father sent Yeshua to help deliver someone from demons, we know that He can send us, too.

Also, there was a storm that whipped up intensely during the boat ride across the sea. This was most likely a demonic spirit sent to stop Yeshua from getting to the other side. When Yeshua commanded it to be still, it obeyed Him. We see something similar happening in the Book of Job. Here, satan used similar natural disasters to attack Job and cause him grief, including lightning and a great wind across the desert (probably a sandstorm) (Job 1). Knowing that satan can use natural disasters like this is something we must consider when rebuking demon spirits. If Yeshua rebuked a storm, then the Lord may ask us to rebuke one as well, or something similar. Something to be aware of and to be ready for. Yeshua said we would do the things He was doing and greater (John 14:12).

The disciples were astonished by this miracle and said to one another, "Who is this Man? Even the wind and waves obey his Word." (Matthew 8:27)

Additionally, the storm came on suddenly. From my own experience with the demonic, when something comes on suddenly, (a storm, a disease, odd physical symptoms, an unlikely bad situation) it most certainly is demonic warfare. The Scripture says the storm came on suddenly and was ferocious – to the point the disciples who were full grown men, thought they were going to die (Mark 4:39). It must have been fierce. Again, something to be aware of. If your child suddenly has a tummy pain, think deeper before you run for Pepto Bismol. If the pain moves quickly from your child's head to his tummy, and then his side, jumping from place to place, it is most certainly a demonic spirit (speaking from experience). First, ask the Lord if you or the family should repent of any sin. Repent of anything that comes to mind. Then if you feel led, rebuke the symptom or pain in Yeshua's name. When we have done this, the various pains that have come on quickly also left quickly. Hallelujah! You may wonder why we would repent of sin first. Because of this verse,

So then, surrender to God. Stand up to the devil and resist
him and he will flee in agony. (James 4:7)

We have learned the hard way that unrepented sin can open doors to the demonic. If a demon is rebuked, but the sin is left unrepented, the demon(s) can keep coming back and often, will make things worse. If you are being harassed by the demonic, especially on a regular basis, ask the Lord if it is related to any sin in your life or that of a family member. Make sure to repent of any sin, then rebuke the demon(s). Afterward, address any changes in your home or life that need to be made. Over the years, the Lord has guided us away from certain holidays, TV shows, video games, and related items in our home. He showed us these things were opening doors to the demonic. We repented of our involvement in these things and made the necessary changes quickly. In turn, the demonic attacks stopped. Praise God! Remember, satan wants to devour us. He is not playing patty cake. We must not have anything in common with him.

Be well balanced and always alert, because your enemy,
the devil, roams around incessantly, like a roaring lion
looking for its prey to devour. (1 Peter 5:8)

I won't speak with you much longer, for the ruler of this
*dark world is coming. But he has no power over me, **for***
he has nothing to use against me. (John 14:30)

A final nugget from this passage is that satan will often send opposition our way when we are being sent by the Lord to do good. Remember, satan is like a roaring lion looking for prey to devour (1 Peter 5:8). Things don't always go smoothly just because we are sent by God. In this passage, Yeshua was clearly sent by His Father to the other side of the sea. As He was obeying, warfare hit (the fierce storm). But Yeshua did not back down or turn the boat around. He simply commanded the storm to stop. In Aramaic, He said,

"Peace. Submit to the will of God." (Mark 4:39)

The storm stopped instantly. Yeshua then continued to the other side of the sea. As Paul so eloquently put it, opportunities often come with opposition (below verse summarized). May we all be aware of this concept and not back down because of opposition from the enemy.

There's an amazing door of opportunity standing wide
open for me to minister here, even though there are many
who oppose and stand against me. (1 Corinthians 16:9)

A Fever Gone in Sixty Seconds

Years ago, after realizing Yeshua gave believers the authority to rebuke and cast out demons, I began to practice here and there on my family whenever I felt there was a demon manifesting. Sounds a little crazy, I know, but stay with me. One day, my son who was probably eight-years-old at the time, had come down with some type of cold or flu. He had a fever all day. Frustrated about this illness and wanting my son to be whole, I remembered the passage in Scripture where Yeshua cast out a demon from Peter's mother-in-law that was manifesting as a fever (Luke 4:39). I felt led to go for it. So, placing my hand on my son's head, I commanded the fever to go in the name of Jesus. Within sixty seconds or less, my son sat up and asked for food! The demon left and so did the fever. He was miraculously healed. Glory to God!

> *Jesus stood over her and rebuked the fever, and she was healed instantly. Then she got up and began to serve them.*
> (Luke 4:39)

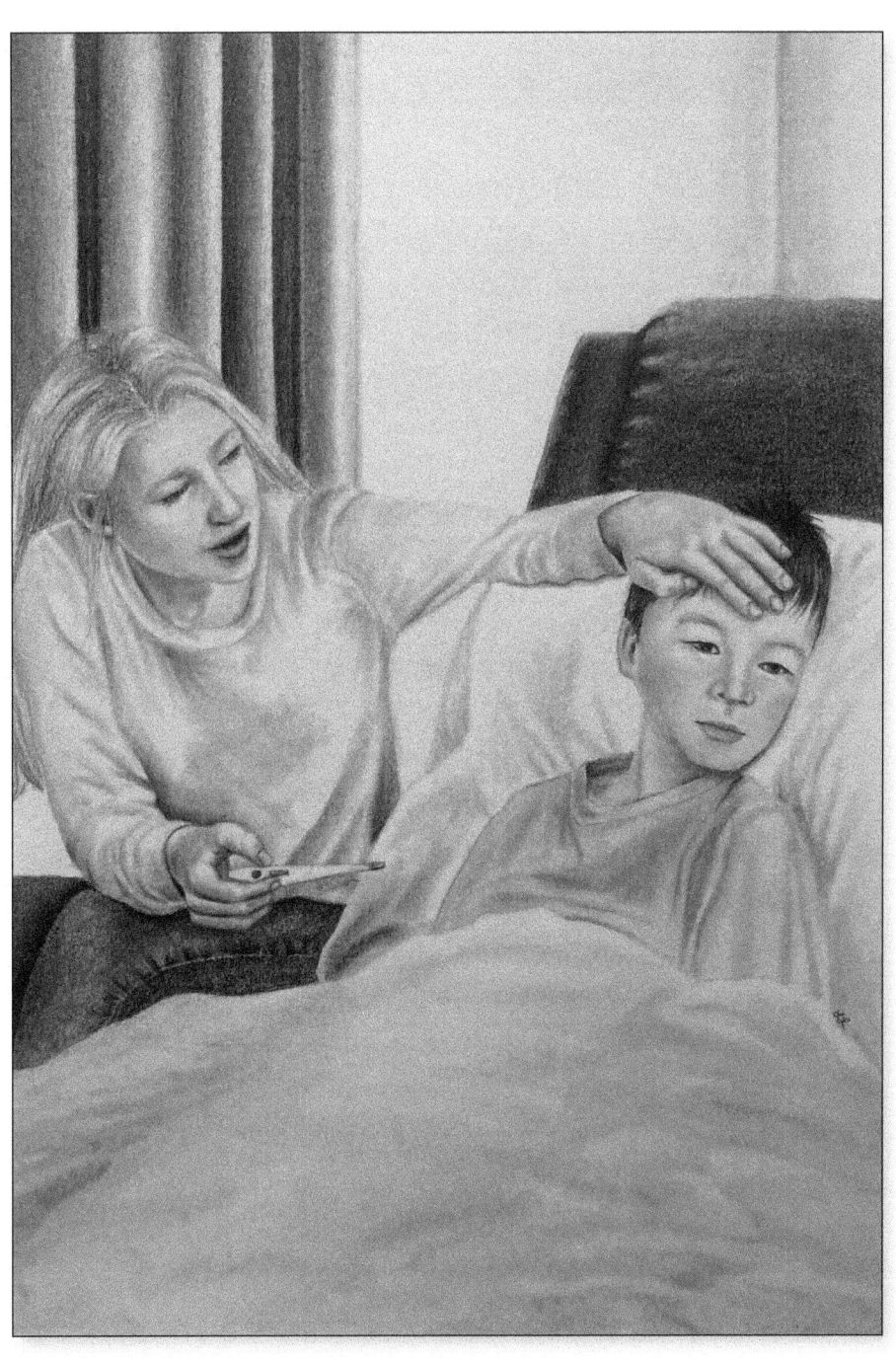

A Fever Gone in Sixty Seconds

Night Time Terror and Mama-Bear

One night about a year ago, my son Zachariah came into the bedroom whispering that he needed some help spiritually. Instantly, I knew this meant he was being attacked by something from the demonic. Sam and I have taught the children how to address the demonic on their own with the power of Yeshua, but at times, they still come to us for help, and we are happy to assist. It is so important that we train our children to walk in the authority that Yeshua has given us.

> It is so important that we train our children to walk in the authority that Yeshua has given us.

Knowing that unconfessed sin can be an open door for the demonic, I asked my son if there was anything he needed to repent of. Zach told me right away that he was afraid of something. Leading him in a quick prayer of repentance for being afraid, we walked quickly over to his bedroom. At this point, I was in mama-bear mode thinking,

How dare that foul-lying-devil keep my child up at night! This thing must go now!

Marching into my son's bedroom, Zach close behind, I could feel the heaviness all over in the room. It's hard to explain, but sometimes you can just feel the ugliness of the demonic. In full-blown mama-bear mode now, the Holy Spirit started speaking through me,

"In the name of Jesus, I take authority over all the power of darkness and satan himself and command you to leave now! And I forbid you to return!"

By the third or fourth word, that demon flew out of Zach's room so fast! I'm sure it saw us coming, and it knew Zach's repentance meant it could not torment him any longer. Thank you, Yeshua for the authority You have given us believers!

> *Now you understand that I have imparted to you my authority to trample over his kingdom.* ***You will trample upon every demon before you and overcome every power Satan possesses.*** *Absolutely nothing will harm you as you walk in this authority.* (Luke 10:19)

Quick note: I have successfully rebuked the demonic in Jesus' name and also in Yeshua's name. The demonic knows Whose authority I am speaking in – and they flee.

Too Quick at the Draw

Now let's touch on the timing of rebuking demons. This was something the Lord needed to teach me. About five years ago, our daughter was diagnosed with three terrible cases of epilepsy. This news came on suddenly and was on the heels of our first miscarriage. This was also a season where the whole family was drawing closer to the Lord, and it felt like satan was working overtime to slow us down. Knowing satan likes to devour believers (1 Peter 5:8), we sought council from the Holy Spirit. He guided us to the story in the Bible where Yeshua rebuked a demon out of a boy with epilepsy and the demon and the epilepsy left the boy and he was made whole (Mark 9). From this testimony in Scripture, the Lord showed us that epilepsy was a demonic spirit. Now we understood that we were not just dealing with a sickness, but a demonic spirit too.

We decided to approach our daughter's situation from all angles. We gave her pharmaceutical medication prescribed by the doctors, and we also prayed for a miraculous healing from the Lord. As the months continued and she showed no improvement, we followed healing Scriptures from the Bible. We laid hands on her for healing. We put oil on her and took her to various elders for prayer (James 5:14-16). We even fasted and prayed (Mark 9:29). In addition, we kept rebuking the demon of epilepsy again and again. No matter what we did though, things kept getting worse.

At the time, she was about three years old and had not yet accepted Yeshua as her Savior. We had not explained salvation to her because we thought she was too young to understand. Over time however, we began to realize strange demonic forces present in her. Her eyes would often become very dark and she would say dark things that did not sound like her personality or character at all!

About that time, the Lord highlighted the following passage to me:

When a demon is cast out of a person, it goes to wander in a waterless realm, searching for rest. But finding no place to rest, it says, "I will go back and reoccupy the body I left."

When it returns, it finds the person like a house swept clean and made tidy, but empty. Then it goes and enlists seven demons more evil than itself, and they all enter and possess the person, leaving that one in a much worse state than before. (Luke 11:24-26)

From these verses, I realized that by my desperate attempts to try everything and anything from Scripture to heal our baby girl, including casting out the demonic time and time again, I had made things worse! Now our sweet daughter had lots of crazy demonic activity going on *in addition* to the epileptic seizures. Before I continue, please realize that everything we were doing by faith was Biblical, and I am not discounting any of it (fasting, oil, prayer for healing, rebuking demons, and so forth). But in everything, we are to be led by the Holy Spirit. That is the part I was missing. I did not realize this back then, so I was doing everything and anything I could think of in my own strength, instead of following the Holy Spirit's lead.

> In everything, we are to be led by the Holy Spirit.

At the time, several God-fearing people in our lives encouraged us to explain salvation to our daughter even though she was so young. This was the Holy Spirit leading us through wise counsel. After explaining salvation to our daughter, she accepted the Messiah as her Savior, and instantly the demonic forces flew out of her. Her house (heart) was swept clean from the demonic, but this time it was also filled with the Holy Spirit. The demons were no longer allowed to return. Hallelujah!

Later that day she began to sing to the Lord. Her countenance was gentle, and the dark eyes were completely gone. As she sang about Yeshua, she even began to dance and twirl like a normal little girl again. Astonished, I remember thinking she was *"dressed and in her right mind."* (Mark 5:15a) I have never seen such supernatural transformation in my life. We continued to pray, and then about a year later, the Lord came in a supernatural whirlwind and miraculously healed our daughter of epilepsy. It is an amazing story that I go into detail with in my first book, but she is healed and whole to this day. All glory to God! He restored our baby girl, and we will never stop thanking Him and praising His name!

Please learn from me though – timing is key. Yeshua knew what He was talking about in Luke 11 regarding how demons operate. He was warning us not to be too quick-at-the-draw. He wants the demons out of course, but at the same time, He knows people's hearts. If they are not born-again believers or they *are* believers in Him, but are not ready to repent of certain sin, then casting demons out pre-maturely will only make things worse for them. Our rebuke may temporarily sweep their house (heart) clean, but it does not put anything in its place, so demons are allowed to return and bring more evil demons with. I hope this all makes sense, if not, please reread this section. This is a key concept that has helped me regarding demonic deliverance – only rebuke the demonic from someone if the Holy Spirit is leading you to.

Just be careful is what I'm saying, but don't freeze up. Follow the Spirit. If you feel repentance is necessary prior to rebuking the demon, do that. If not, then don't. One time, I felt led to disciple the person with Bible studies after rebuking the demonic. Whatever the Holy Spirit guides you to do, do that.

> **Only rebuke the demonic from someone if the Holy Spirit is leading you to.**

Also, if you feel *you* are the one needing deliverance, you can do it yourself or grab a friend who loves the Lord to help you. Ask the Lord why the attacks or harassment is happening. If He guides you to change or repent of something in your life, do it. It could be something from your past or childhood. So, make sure to think through things carefully, and repent of anything that may be an open door. Then command the demon(s) to go in Yeshua's name! My family and I have done this over the years as needed, and the demonic spirits have left. When we submit to the Father and resist the devil, the devil does flee. Glory to God!

> *So then, surrender to God. Stand up to the devil and resist him and he will flee in agony.* (James 4:7)

Chapter 14

Led to Raise the Dead

I n Matthew 10:7-8, Yeshua told His followers to do many things while they were out sharing the gospel. One of them was to raise the dead. We see followers of Yeshua raising people from the dead in the Old Testament with Elijah and Elisha (1 Kings 17 and 2 Kings 4) and also in the New Testament with Peter (Acts 9).

When God created the earth, He created Adam and Eve not to die. However, as soon as they disobeyed Him, their bodies began to deteriorate and die. This is how death entered the world (Romans 5:12). At times, people pass away earlier than they should due to an accident, an illness, or something else untimely. As Yeshua walked the earth, we see a few instances where He was led to raise certain people back to life. Abba's desire is for all of us to accomplish everything the Lord wrote about us in our book (Psalm 139:16). He does not want us to die early.

> *Therefore, just as sin came into the world through one man, and death through sin, so death spread to all people, because they all sinned.* (Romans 5:12 AMP)

Before Yeshua ascended into Heaven and sat down at the right hand of the Father, He gave His followers many commands. The greatest, of course, is to love the Lord with all our hearts. The second is to love others as we love ourselves (Mark 12:29-31). But there are many others commands from Scripture that we can obey to show Abba that we love Him. We have touched on many of them already (heal the sick, cast out the demonic, and so on), but now let's focus on raising the dead. First, let's see what we can glean from Scripture, and then we'll talk about personal experiences.

Here, Yeshua is instructing His followers:

> *And as you go, preach this message: 'Heaven's kingdom realm is accessible, close enough to touch.'*

> *You must continually bring healing to lepers and to those who are sick, and make it your habit to break off the demonic presence from people, **and raise the dead back to life**. Freely you have received the power of the kingdom, so freely release it to others.* (Matthew 10:7-8)

The Lord's desire is for His followers to do all these things, modeling His life on earth. Now let's see how Peter (one of Yeshua's followers) obeyed Yeshua's commands.

Peter Helps a Seamstress

After Yeshua ascended into Heaven, Peter ministered in a city called Lydda. He had recently healed a man there who was bedridden for many years and was paralyzed. Here is what Scripture says:

Peter said to him, "Aeneas, Jesus the Anointed One instantly and divinely heals you. Now, get up and make your bed." (Acts 9:34)

I love the passion and authority that Peter walked in, showing others Yeshua's love. The Scripture says many came to salvation because of this man's healing. Right after this wonderful miracle, about fifteen or twenty miles away in a city named Joppa, a very kind, God-fearing disciple of Yeshua named Tabitha had passed away from an illness. Scripture explains that she was a maker of many tunics and garments to bless others (a seamstress). Many of the disciples were mourning her death, but when they heard Peter was nearby in Lydda, they sent two disciples to get him. He came at once. After asking everyone to leave the room, he knelt down and prayed.

Peter Helps a Seamstress

Then he turned to her dead body and said,

"Tabitha, rise up!"

Scripture says she came back to life immediately and sat up. And because of this resurrection from the dead, many people in Joppa gave their lives to the Messiah (Acts 9:32-42). Glory to God! Peter was absolutely following in Yeshua's footsteps.

> *But the love of God will be perfected within the one who obeys God's Word. We can be sure that we've truly come to live in intimacy with God, not just by saying, "I am intimate with God," but by walking in the footsteps of Jesus.* (1 John 2:5-6)

John Lopez & James Lopez

My husband and I are extremely blessed to have healthy children on earth, and feel led by the Lord to have more. However, during our journey over the years to expand our family, we have endured many losses. John Lopez and James Lopez are two of our sons that died in my womb. I was about twelve or thirteen weeks pregnant when John's heart stopped beating, and I was about thirty-seven weeks pregnant when I labored and delivered James (stillborn). In both cases, their hearts just stopped beating. In both cases, we desired them to come back to life. Both times we prayed for resurrection from the dead.

John passed back in 2019, and James passed in 2022. In both cases, as you can imagine, we were overcome with grief and very emotional. Both times as we prayed for resurrection, my husband and I just thought we were obeying the command of the Lord in Scripture to raise the dead (Matthew 10:8). We assumed we were acting in accordance with the will of God.

About six months after James passed, still grieving, looking for answers, I went before the Lord and began asking questions. Something wasn't right. Per the above passage in Scripture and other examples in Scripture where believers raised the dead, it certainly seemed we were obeying the Lord in praying for resurrection for our boys. My thoughts stumbled together,

God told us to raise the dead. We had faith. We believed. What happened?

My questions continued as I reflected on the fact that back in 2019 when I miscarried John, my father received a dream where the Lord told him,

"Tell her to trust My decision." Meaning I was to trust the Father's decision in allowing this miscarriage, to accept it, and to let go.

Then in 2022 I gave birth to James, almost full-term. Holding him in my arms (7 pounds, 19 inches), we prayed for God to bring him back to life, but I could hear the Holy Spirit saying,

"Let go." Again, God was saying no. I was so confused and broken-hearted. Still grieving months later, my thoughts to the Lord continued…

Father, why in Scripture have You commanded us to raise the dead, yet in real life when we have tried, Your answer was no?

It seemed like an out-right contradiction. The answer to this very question is how the Lord inspired me to write this book. His answer was simple and direct.

> *For as many as are led by the Spirit of God, these are sons of God.* (Romans 8:14 NKJV)

As Holy Spirit dropped this verse into my spirit, a spark of revelation flooded my heart, and my mind began to race. For years, I thought followers of Yeshua were *always* to attempt to heal the sick, raise the dead and so on (Matthew 10:8 and Mark 16:17-18). I thought this was obedience to God's Word.

What are You saying, Lord? Even if You command me in Scripture to raise the dead, I'm still to be led by Your Spirit? Is this why the boys didn't come back, because You weren't leading us to raise them from the dead?

The impression was, *Yes.*

My former understanding of these Scriptures started to crumble as the Lord's truth kept flooding my heart.

Wait...does this apply to all *imperative commands in Scripture, Lord? (*imperative commands ie: preach the gospel, heal the sick, cleanse the leper, and raise the dead)

Again, the impression was, *Yes.*

My mind began reeling as I analyzed Romans 8:14 further. Had the Holy Spirit actually *led* me to raise James from the dead? Looking back on it... no... He hadn't. I even asked my husband later on. Same answer. No, Sam didn't receive a personal Word from the Lord or an impression to try either. We were both just really wanting our precious baby boy to come back to life, and we felt like we were obeying the verses in Scripture to raise the dead. It was the same situation I believe years earlier with John. My mama heart desperately wanted him back, but I had no clear memory of the Holy Spirit leading us to pray for resurrection for him either.

The downloads kept coming as I thought about healing others. Had Yeshua *asked* me to lay hands for healing on all the people I'd attempted to heal over the years? No, He hadn't. Some of them, yes, and they were healed! Praise the Lord! But the same could apply for demonic deliverance as well. Was I led every single time? I don't think so. In my compassion or desire to see the person come back to life or be made whole, at times, I sailed right past the check point with Holy Spirit, thinking I was already obeying God's Word. But the Passion translation says it this way:

> The **mature** children of God are those (and only those) who are moved by the impulses of the Holy Spirit. (Romans 8:14)

The mature part was key. If I wanted to be mature in the Lord, my ability to sense the impulses of the Holy Spirit would need to increase.

For years I had wondered about the disparity in how Yeshua was successful every time He would heal someone, or raise them from the dead, but I was not always successful. The Lord was gently teaching me that I needed to mature. I needed to be led by the Holy Spirit, in everything.

> The Holy Spirit was showing me the next step in maturity was to be led by Him in all things.

Just to be clear, I do not believe it is a sin to attempt to heal someone or to pray for resurrection from the dead (Matthew 10:8 and Mark 16:17-18). However, as we grow and mature in the Lord, we want to become more effective for the Lord. We want to bear richer and greater fruit for Him, yes? The Holy Spirit was showing me the next step in maturity was to be led by Him in all things.

I am the true Vine, and My Father is the vinedresser. Every branch in Me that does not bear fruit, He takes away; and every branch that continues to bear fruit, He [repeatedly] prunes, so that it will bear more fruit [even richer and finer fruit]. (John 15:1-2 AMP)

After this encounter with the Lord, He led me to some Scripture where various followers of Yeshua were rerouted by Holy Spirit as they attempted to obey the commands in Scripture. In this recent season with James, the Holy Spirit's guidance for us was *not* to raise him from the dead but to let go. The impulse of the Holy Spirit for Apostle Peter must have been, *"Go for it!"* or something similar, because Tabitha came back from the dead (Acts 9). Hallelujah!

Later in the Book of Acts, we see the impulse of the Holy Spirit for Paul was not to go to certain places to preach the gospel. Holy Spirit actually stopped him from preaching in certain places. Then He rerouted Paul to Macedonia (Acts 16). Even though Paul was attempting to obey a command in Scripture to preach the gospel, the Holy Spirit stopped him. Just like He stopped us from raising James from the dead. Because Paul didn't force it, but submitted to Holy Spirit's leading to Macedonia, the Father was blessed, and many were saved. Results followed Paul as he followed Holy Spirit.

As we submitted to the Father, and let go of John and James on earth, we have seen immense fruit come from our trust and submission to the Lord. We have much compassion for others going through similar loss, and we also have learned not to hold on so tightly to this world anymore. By God's grace, even in sorrow, we have been able to give Him the glory.

*He always comes alongside us to comfort us in every suf-
fering so that we can come alongside those who are in any
painful trial. We can bring them this same comfort that
God has poured out upon us.* (2 Corinthians 1:4)

*The person who loves his life and pampers himself will
miss true life! But the one who detaches his life from this
world and abandons himself to me, will find true life and
enjoy it forever!* (John 12:25)

Dreams of Resurrection from the Dead

A month or two ago, the Lord gave me two dreams of resurrection
from the dead. I believe He gave these dreams to me to explain and
clear up further questions I had regarding how it looks and feels to
raise someone from the dead. I realize what I'm about to share are just
dreams, but if you're open to it, I believe they will bless and encourage
you as well.

The first dream was of Sam and I in a different country, training
a group of kids that were about ten to fourteen-years-old. We were
teaching them how to race small cars around a race track. This is
strange, I know. We were not in America. This was a foreign country
I could tell. Dirt track, nothing fancy or very clean. I kept some newer
children close to me in order to teach them how to drive well.

As I glanced over to see how Sam was doing with his group of kids,
I noticed one of the newer girls he was working with was getting away
from him. It was obvious she was not submitting to his instructions. I
was sad and concerned all at once thinking she might hurt or kill herself

from recklessness on the track. Just then, she drove off the track. She was going too fast, ignoring Sam's guidance. There were no guardrails on the track, just a dirt track with grass or gravel on the outer part. So, you *could* go outside the track, but it would be very rough and hard to control. As I watched her drive outside the track, my thoughts were,

No, I don't want her to die!

Aggressively driving, she pushed her way back onto the track, but this pushed a boy driver completely out of the race causing him to die on impact. This is a strange and violent dream, I know, but please stay with me. I looked and saw him slumped over, dead, next to his vehicle. Now please pay attention to my reaction. This was my biggest take away to raising the dead from this dream.

I was instantly crushed with grief. My heart screamed,

No, no, no! This cannot be happening.

Overcome with such internal sadness, I ran to his side, praying for resurrection. He was no more than ten or twelve-years-old. Sam came too. I sensed he came to agree for resurrection. Then the girl came around and I thought,

No Lord, no. She will be overcome with grief at what she has caused. It was as though she didn't realize he was dead yet.

My thoughts raced in anguish,

It cannot end this way for her either God – how will she live with herself?

She was only twelve or so herself. I may have seen some movement in his arm, but I wasn't sure. So, I grabbed his hand and prayed and prayed to the Lord for him not to be dead. I was saying things like,

"Breath! Please breath!"

I remember looking up to the sky in the dream and crying out,

"Please Lord, please let him live!"

I thought I saw a little movement again. This time I did! Then he sat right up, totally healed and whole! Praise Adonia! The first words out of his mouth were something about forgiveness to the girl who caused it. Wow! He wasn't angry at all. I was astounded and relieved all at the same time. My heaviness started to lift. Looking into the clouds, I raised my hand to Heaven and said something like,

"Thank you, Yahweh!!!!"

Then I awoke.

As I reflected on this dream, the Lord highlighted my deep compassion for the boy and the girl. He also showed me it only took thirty seconds to a minute. The impression was,

Katie, you will just know when to raise someone from the dead – your deep compassion and urgency will take over and it will happen quickly.

> As I reflected on this dream, the Lord highlighted
> my deep compassion for the boy and the girl.

This cleared up my confusion on how long (how many hours/days) one must pray for resurrection. Unless you are directed by the Holy Spirit to pray longer, I believe it should happen quickly. From Scriptural accounts and from the dream, the moment a person started praying for resurrection or commanding the person to come back, the dead person came back quickly, within a couple minutes or less (John 11:43-44, Acts 9:40, and Acts 20:9-10).

And when I say I had huge compassion, it was like my heart was going to fall out of my chest. My heaviness for this needing to be un-done was more than anything I had ever experienced in real life, even with both our boys. I'm not sure if this is what each one of us will experience if Abba asks us to raise the dead, I'm simply sharing what I felt and understood from the dream God gave me. I just knew in my gut things could not end like this. And glory to God they did not.

11 Shortly afterward, Jesus left on a journey to the village of Nain, with a massive crowd of people following him, and his disciples.

12 As he approached the village, he met a multitude of people in a funeral procession, who were mourning as they carried the body of a young man to the cemetery. The boy was his mother's only son, and she was a widow.

*13 When the Lord saw the grieving mother, **his heart broke for her***. With great tenderness he said to her, "Please don't cry."*

14 Then he stepped up to the coffin and touched it. When the pallbearers came to a halt, Jesus spoke directly to the corpse, "Young man, I say to you, arise and live!"

15 Immediately, the young man moved, sat up, and spoke to those nearby. Jesus presented the son to his mother, alive!

16 A tremendous sense of holy mystery swept over the crowd. They shouted praises to God, saying, "God himself has blessed us by visiting his people! A great prophet has appeared among us!" (Luke 7:11-16)

*The Greek word for "**His heart broke for her**" is splanch-nizomai. The Passion Translation says this is the deepest level of compassion. It says there is no greater word in the Greek language to describe the depth of emotion Jesus felt for this widow over the loss of her son. That is what I believe I was feeling for both the boy and the girl in the dream. My mama heart was aching for their wholeness, physically and emotionally.*

Another dream I had about a month ago was similar, but had a new angle. Again, I believe the Lord was using this dream to train me and teach me about resurrection from the dead.

Myself and many others were in a big church setting. Not all the seats were filled, but there were about fifty of us in a big room. I understood that a teen or young twenty-something had passed away. It wasn't clear in the dream if she passed away right there in the service, or prior. It was recent though. It wasn't clear in my spirit whether I should go and pray for her right then, so I did not. Then a woman near me said something about having faith to raise her from the dead.

I told her I would go with her and agree with her in faith. She and I both turned to go to the young woman who had passed. I must have been walking slowly because by the time I entered the room, the woman with faith had already prayed for the young woman and she had come back to life! Praise Adonai!

What I gleaned from this dream was that I do not always have to be the one to raise the dead. Others can, and I can simply agree with them in faith. Also, it happened quickly in this dream as well. She or we did not have to pray for hours or days for resurrection. Again, we cannot put God in a box, it could take longer. But in both dreams, the resurrection happened quickly. The resurrection stories in Scripture also happened quickly. Once someone started praying for resurrection or commanding the dead to be raised, they were raised within seconds or minutes at most (Mark 5:21-43, John 11:1-46, Acts 9:36-43).

I will say there was a distinct difference in the dreams when I felt led to raise the dead and when I felt led to just agree in faith. From that alone, I do believe we will have a clear nudge what to do. May we all lean on the Holy Spirit and allow Him to guide us, even in raising the dead.

> *He tenderly clasped the child's hand in his and said to her in Aramaic, "Talitha koum," which means, "Little girl, wake up from the sleep of death." Instantly the twelve-year-old girl sat up, stood to her feet, and started walking around the room! Everyone was overcome with astonishment in seeing this miracle!* (Mark 5:41-42)

Chapter 15

Being a Mature Child of God

Knowing our stay on earth is growing short, it is important we spend our time wisely. There are many productive things we can be involved in like Bible studies, feeding the homeless, helping in children's ministry, or other wonderful things. There are many people we can pray for healing and rebuke the demonic from. But over the years, and especially in this recent season of my life, I have learned not to do good things just for the sake of doing good things (checking the box).

When we do good works on our own, without being led by the Holy Spirit, we can often wear ourselves out. However, when we are led by the Holy Spirit to do good works, it never seems to lead to exhaustion and our obedience bears great fruit for the Kingdom of Heaven. This is a sign of maturity. The Lord wants to lead us daily to accomplish these good works (Ephesians 2:10). He puts certain people in our lives that He wants us to break the demonic off of, to bless, to heal, or even to raise from the dead.

> *For we are His workmanship, created in Christ Jesus **for good works**, which God prepared beforehand, so that we would walk in them.* (Ephesians 2:10 AMP)

What the Lord has planned for you may not look like what He has planned for someone else. But no matter how lonely the path may seem, no matter the trials we face, we must let the Holy Spirit lead us in these good works. Often, what He asks us to do is interwoven with other people's lives, and our obedience or disobedience affects them directly.

> *You are the body of the Anointed One, and each of you is a unique and vital part of it.* (1 Corinthians 12:27)

> **Often, what He asks us to do is interwoven with other people's lives, and our obedience or disobedience affects them directly.**

Worship in Spirit and in Truth

Before we close out this chapter with additional examples of being led by the Holy Spirit, let me remind you (and myself) that Yeshua mentions a very serious thing regarding judgement day. He says **many** will arrive and will say to Him,

"Lord, Lord"

…but He will have to send them away. They will mention doing miracles, casting out the demonic, and so on – *in Yeshua's name*. How is this possible? Based on Scripture, there are people who work these miracles, but do not persist in doing the will of the Father (Matthew 7:21-23). Yeshua tells these people to depart from Him, that He never knew them because they were lawless rebels (not obeying God's Law) which also indicates a rebellious spirit. Not good.

*Not everyone who says to me, "Lord, Lord," will enter into heaven's kingdom. It is **only those who persist in doing the will of my heavenly Father.***

*On the day of judgment **many** will say to me, "Lord, Lord, don't you remember us? Didn't we prophesy in your name? Didn't we cast out demons and do many miracles in your name?" But I will have to say to them, "Go away from me, you **lawless rebels**! I've never been joined to you!"* (Matthew 7:21-23)

So, although these folks were moving in the gifts of the Spirit, they were not persistently doing the will of the Father. The will of the Father is written all over the Bible – Old and New Testament. Yeshua says His Word *is* truth (John 17:17). To find His truth, we must be diligent to read our Bibles (entirely, not just the New Testament) and obey what the Father commands us to do.

*God is spirit, and those who worship Him must worship **in spirit and truth.*** (John 4:24 AMP)

> **As mature children of God, may we be Spirit led, but also lovers of God's truth, reading and obeying His Word daily.**

Although the emphasis of this book is being led by the Holy Spirit, we must also worship God in truth (John 4:24). God's Word is truth (John 17:17). In my quiet time with the Father, I often read a chapter in the Old Testament and a chapter in the New Testament. Then I use a Strongs Concordance to look up hard words or anything that seems contradicting or confusing. Remember, the Strongs Concordance tells us the original Greek or Hebrew definition of the word that was translated into English. Many times, the seeming contradiction is cleared up by discovering the original Greek or Hebrew meaning of the word(s). This helps me find and do the will of the Father. And as a heads up, the will of the Father according to Scripture, does not always line up with main stream Christianity teachings or traditions. So, please side with God's Word vs. your friend, pastor, or relative who claim they are reading God's Word, but are not reading it carefully. As a mature follower of Messiah, you are responsible for doing the will of the Father – whether your church, family, or friends are obeying Him or not. We are individually held accountable.

> *Therefore, each one must answer for himself and give a personal account of his own life before God.* (Romans 14:12)

Remember, we must be self-feeders of God's Word, His truth. We should not rely on our pastor or others believers to tell us what God's Word says. As mature children of God, may we be Spirit led, but also lovers of God's truth, reading and obeying His Word daily. No lawlessness allowed. And to be clear, we are not reading and obeying God's Word to earn our salvation. Salvation is a gift of God, received by faith in the Messiah. Not by works (Ephesians 2:8-9). We obey God and persistently do His will because we love Him. Yeshua's love language is obedience.

> **If you [really] love Me**, *you will keep and obey My commandments.* (John 14:15 AMP)

> We obey God and persistently do His will because we love Him. Yeshua's love language is obedience.

My delight is found in all your laws, and I won't forget to walk in your words. (Psalm 119:16)

Examples of Being Led

As we wrap up our time together, I want to leave you with a few more examples of how the Holy Spirit has led me and my family over the years. As you read along, try to identify if Holy Spirit has spoken to you in a similar manner, or perhaps you will hear something new that will help you as well. I'm always excited when I discover new ways the Holy Spirit can speak to us. I hope these examples encourage you as we all seek maturity in being led by the Holy Spirit.

Many of these styles can be found in 1 Corinthians 12. Often, the Holy Spirit will flash the future to me in various ways. He does not yell. It's more like an impression or a picture in my mind of something to come. If the flash includes me doing or saying something to someone, as I obey, I usually see fruit right away and more flashes and nudges keep coming. When I have chosen *not* to obey in the moment, or put certain things off for a day or two, fewer nudges seem to come from Him. It is almost like Holy Spirit needs to see that He can trust me before He gives me more assignments. I don't blame Him and have done my best to increase my quick obedience out of love for the Father (John 14:15).

The one who has [a heart of faithful stewardship] will be given more [to manage]. And the one who has very little [faithfulness, wisdom, integrity] will lose the little he has [failed to manage well]. (Matthew 25:29)

Word of Knowledge – One warm afternoon last year, the family and I were eating at a restaurant. We were seated near a window. As we finished our meal, I glanced out the window and saw a homeless man digging through the trash can out front. The Holy Spirit nudged me to give him our leftovers. Looking quickly at the table, all we really had left was a basket of fries. The impression was,

Yes – give it to him.

Jumping up quickly, I obeyed. The man was so grateful. Praise the Lord!

Word of Knowledge – Another time, I was just leaving a parking lot, driving home from errands when I saw a homeless lady. It was a very hot day in Florida. Holy Spirit seemed to highlight her and remind me I had water bottles in the back of the van. Agreeing in my heart, I pulled over quickly and offered the waters to her, she was *so* grateful. I prayed with her before leaving.

For when you saw me hungry, you fed me. When you found me thirsty, you gave me drink. When I had no place to stay, you invited me in, and when I was poorly clothed, you covered me. When I was sick, you tenderly cared for me, and when I was in prison you visited me. (Matthew 25:35-36)

Word of Knowledge – As I was shopping in Walmart the other day, one of the workers accidentally spilled a very full box of tags. Holy Spirit said inside my heart,

Help her.

Pulling my cart over, I immediately, squatted down and began picking up the tags. Soon after, another worker joined us. She was very thankful for all the help.

Word of Wisdom – Recently I was speaking with my friend over the phone. As she was telling me about the various things going on in her life, it seemed I heard the word, *Move* in my heart. The impression was,

Ask her if she and her husband have considered moving out of state.

So, I asked her and told her it seemed to be from the Lord. She immediately said that she and her husband had both been wanting to move. She was very excited and encouraged.

> We must not be afraid. Instead, may we be bold and brave for Abba.

It's important that we speak up when the Holy Spirit guides us. Remember, our lives are woven together with others. The word God gives us (even if it is small) might be the very word that person needs to hear from the Lord. We must not be afraid. Instead, may we be bold and brave for Abba.

For God will never give you the spirit of fear, but the Holy Spirit who gives you mighty power, love, and self-control. (2 Timonthy 1:7)

Wise Council – The Lord can guide us through listening to wise men and women of God. The Lord used friends from my mom's church to lead me and my husband. They guided us in helping Julia accept Yeshua as her Savior even though she was so young at the time. If you remember from the earlier chapter, this forced the demonic to leave her and not to come back.

> *Listen well to wise counsel and be willing to learn from correction so that by the end of your life you'll be known for your wisdom.* (Proverbs 19:20)

Word of Knowledge – Over the summer as I was gearing up for the next school year, the Lord led me to a homeschool robotics and engineering class for our son, Zachariah. As I was looking over the details of the class, the Holy Spirit brought another mom to my mind. Not only is she another homeschooler, but she is also very good in science and math. The impression was,

Give her the information – I want her to know about this class.

I shared it with her. Shortly afterward, she told me she had been praying for wisdom about the school year and felt this was an answer to prayer. Praise God!

> *Each believer is given continuous revelation by the Holy Spirit to benefit not just himself but all.* (1 Corinthians 12:7)

Songs from the Lord – In Scripture, it says the Lord can sing over us (Psalm 32:7). At times, I will hear a song on "replay" in my mind. When this happens, the Holy Spirit has taught me that it is usually the Father or the angels singing over me with a message. When I hear something replaying in my heart, I have learned to start singing along. As I let the words of the song sink into my heart, the message from the Lord usually becomes very clear.

About two years ago, we were still looking for housing and I was about seven months pregnant with James. It had been one of the most challenging seasons of my life with Sam leaving his job by the Lord's direction, no insurance for several months, moving from hotel to hotel, and so on. I was exhausted emotionally and physically. Then one morning I began hearing this old chorus playing in my heart again and again.

> *I just called to say I love you*
> *I just called to say how much I care*
> *I just called to say I love you*
> *And I mean it from the bottom of my heart*

It finally hit me that the Lord was singing a love song over me! He was telling me that He loved me by way of this song. It blessed my socks off! He saw all that I was doing, all that I was going through, and just wanted to "call" and say,

I love you, Katie.

Often, He will sing Biblical songs over me, but this one by Stevie Wonder was perfect! Thank you, Yeshua. I love You too.

> *Lord, you are my secret hiding place, protecting me from*
> *these troubles, **surrounding me with songs of gladness!***
> *Your joyous shouts of rescue release my breakthrough.*
> *Pause in his presence.* (Psalm 32:7)

Double Witness – Before Sam was rehired by the FAA, the Holy Spirit first nudged Sam to apply for the position, then shortly afterward, the Lord gave us a dream of the FAA offering Sam a job. We prayed and prayed in faith, and a few months later, Sam was rehired! We have learned this back-to-back direction is from the Lord (a nudge and then a dream, or other double forms of guidance). He is showing us His clear will in the situation. From here, we agree with what He has shown us and then pray and pray until it comes to pass. Remember, God's will is not automatically done in the earth. We must pray for it to be done.

> We have learned this back-to-back direction is from the Lord. He is showing us His will in the situation.

Your kingdom come, Your will be done on earth as it is in heaven. (Matthew 6:10 AMP)

We can see this double witness with Pharoah's two dreams in the Old Testament where Joseph calls it one-and-the-same dream from the Lord. And it certainly did come to pass (Genesis 41:25). Another place in Scripture is where Abraham is promised many descendants and then much later, the Lord comes and tells Abraham that Sarah will have a son this time next year. Issaac *does* arrive within that year (Genesis 15:5 and Genesis 18:10). Later in Hebrews 11, we read that Abraham and Sarah did not give up on God's promises. They had faith.

So whenever we receive a double witness from the Lord, whether a dream, a word of knowledge, or something else from Him, we do our best to pray and keep on praying with faith until it comes to pass in the earth.

*So I say to you, **ask and keep on asking**, and it will be given to you; seek and keep on seeking, and you will find; knock and keep on knocking, and the door will be opened to you.*

For everyone who keeps on asking [persistently], receives; and he who keeps on seeking [persistently], finds; and to him who keeps on knocking [persistently], the door will be opened. (Luke 11:9-10 AMP)

Word of Knowledge – Last year, my husband and I were at the grocery store together. My husband mentioned how hot it was in the store. Outside, it was an extra hot summer day in Florida, with lots of humidity to boot. Because of this, the AC was not exactly running tip-top inside the building. As we brought our items up front, I noticed the young cashier was sweating up a storm. In my heart I felt like I heard,

Drink.

Then the impression was to offer her a drink. At first, she seemed hesitant to tell me her favorite drink not wanting to bother me. But knowing I had heard from the Lord, I encouraged her. She finally smiled and replied,

"I do like the red Gatorades."

Leaving Sam to finish checking out, I quickly located a red Gatorade from the fridge section, paid for it, and ran it over to her. She appreciated it. Hallelujah!

To one is given through the Spirit the message of wisdom,
and to another the word of knowledge and understanding
according to the same Spirit; (1 Corinthians 12:8)

Warning Dreams – Several months ago, I woke from a warning dream about my friend's child. The Lord had shown me a plan of the enemy to take the child's life including the exact method satan was going to use. I felt led right away to call the mother. She agreed it was a scheme of the devil and she and her husband and I prayed against it in Yeshua's name. We put the blood of Yeshua over their sweet daughter, and forbid satan or anything in the darkness to take her life or to hurt her. To this day she is healthy and fine. Thank you, Father!

> *Receive this truth: Whatever you forbid on earth will*
> *be considered to be forbidden in heaven, and whatever*
> *you release on earth will be considered to be released*
> *in heaven.*
>
> *Again, I give you an eternal truth: If two of you agree to*
> *ask God for something in a symphony of prayer, my heav-*
> *enly Father will do it for you. For wherever two or three*
> *come together in honor of my name, I am right there with*
> *them!* (Matthew 18:18-20)

Visions – My oldest two children often have visions. My son closes his eyes and can see in the Spirit, while my daughter has had open visions with color and movement. About five years ago, as I sat in the doctor's office, crying after receiving the news that Baby John passed (our first miscarriage), my oldest son Zachariah, held my hand and said,

"Momma, I can see Yeshua with the baby right now. He is holding the baby. It's ok, Momma. The baby is with Yeshua."

Zachariah's vision from the Lord brought me such comfort that day. So please be open to the Holy Spirit using visions to guide, comfort, or direct us.

> *It shall come about after this that I shall pour out My Spirit on all mankind; and your sons and your daughters will prophesy, your old men will dream dreams, **your young men will see visions**.* (Joel 2:28 AMP)

Hearing in the Spirit – Over the years, the Lord has allowed me to hear various things in the Spirit that were not in the natural realm like a door shutting, a gate opening, a shofar blowing, an angel speaking, a demon screaming, and so on. The day I miscarried Baby Esther (our second miscarriage), I heard a demon screaming in the Spirit. You may think this is harsh for the Lord to allow me to hear this on top of all the physical and emotional pain I was already going through, but it actually helped. The following week when the doctor confirmed the miscarriage, he found no physical cause for it. Because of the demonic scream I heard earlier in the Spirit, I knew the cause was related to something demonic (spiritual warfare), not physical. The Lord helped me look at the miscarriage on a deeper level so I would know what to do next. So please be aware of sounds that seem real, but are in the Spirit. God can use them to guide and direct us.

> *Your hand-to-hand combat is not with human beings, but with the highest principalities and authorities operating in rebellion under the heavenly realms. For they are a*

powerful class of demon-gods and evil spirits that hold this dark world in bondage. (Ephesians 6:12)

Someone's Name – This would be more of a Word of Knowledge I guess, but it is specific to a person. This is when a person's name just keeps coming up in your spirit day after day, but you're not sure why. When this happens, I have found the Lord usually wants me to reach out to this person or pray for this person. When I have, they often say they were thinking of me as well. At times the Lord will give me a hint about what He wants me to say to them, other times, nothing. At minimum, I have learned to reach out with a text or a phone call. This gets the ball rolling and the Holy Spirit takes it from there. Glory to God.

Numbers – The Lord uses numbers often to guide me. It is usually a repeat number that keeps popping up everywhere on street signs, license plates, the clock, and so on. For me, a repeat number usually means: to look the number up in the Strongs Concordance and see the Greek or Hebrew meaning of the number, a Bible reference (chapter and verse), a date of some sort with significance, or the literal page number in my Bible. It has meant other things as well, but usually one of these things will clue me in to what the Lord is saying with the repeat number.

For example, when I see 222 repeated; for me this usually refers to Daniel 2:22, in which the Lord is telling me He wants me to ask Him to reveal something hidden. I ask Him to show me something hidden, something I am missing. Within a day or two He usually reveals something deep that gives me further direction. I am normally always seeking Him about several topics on any given day, so this direction will normally apply to one or more of these things. Praise Adonai.

It is He who reveals the profound and hidden things; He knows what is in the darkness, and the light dwells with Him. (Daniel 2:22 AMP)

Other numbers mean other things to me. For example, 444 usually means open my Bible, or ask the Lord where to open my Bible and read. He will give me a book, chapter, and verse at times. Also, 711 usually means ask Him for a sign (Isaiah 7:11). There are many more, but please start paying attention to repeat numbers you are seeing. Then ask Abba what they mean. His Spirit will guide you.

Go ahead—ask for a sign from Yahweh, your God. Ask for something big, so miraculous that you will know only God did it! (Isaiah 7:11)

Still Small Voice – There are many ways we can see, hear, and sense the leading of the Holy Spirit. Most of the time however, the Holy Spirit speaks to me in a soft voice inside my heart. I ask Him questions, and He answers me. At times, He will join my thoughts, encouraging me, or answering me even before I ask (Matthew 6:8).

Your ears will hear a word behind you, "This is the way, walk in it," whenever you turn to the right or to the left. (Isaiah 30:21 AMP)

In Summary

There are many ways the Holy Spirit can lead and guide us. The examples in this book are certainly not exhaustive, but I hope and pray they have encouraged you. And I pray we all continue to mature as we are led by the Holy Spirit.

> *The **mature** children of God are those who are moved by the impulses of the Holy Spirit.* (Romans 8:14)

> ***Your word** is a lamp to my feet and a light to my path.* (Psalm 119:105 AMP)

> *From now on, worshiping the Father will not be a matter of the right place but with a right heart. For God is a Spirit, and he longs to have sincere worshipers who adore him in the realm of the **Spirit and in truth**.* (John 4:23-24)

Prayer to Receive Salvation

If any of you would like to accept the Messiah as your Savior, follow me in this prayer and really mean it in your heart. You must first repent of your sins, your old way of thinking, sinful habits, and so on. You must truly want to change your life to follow Yeshua. Once you have repented, then believe by faith that Yeshua is Lord and receive His gift of salvation.

"Father, I repent for my sins. Please forgive me and help me to change. Thank you for sending Your Son to die on the cross for my sins. I believe in You. Please come into my heart and life and save me! I invite You to be the Lord of my life."

It is important to realize this decision to follow Yeshua will likely bring persecution from the enemy, however, remember the Lord will be with you and help you. Hold fast to your confession of faith. He is holding fast to you. Find a Bible as soon as you can, and read it often – starting from the beginning. Pray to your Father in heaven often. Ask Him to give you wisdom, and do your best to obey quickly.

And what is God's "living message"? It is the revelation of faith for salvation, which is the message that we preach. For if you publicly declare with your mouth that Jesus is Lord and believe in your heart that God raised him from the dead, you will experience salvation.

The heart that believes in him receives the gift of the righ-teousness of God—and then the mouth confesses, resulting in salvation. (Romans 10:9-10)